MW01101215

Professional Wedding Planning Advice

Featuring 15 interviews with wedding professionals from the Dallas/Fort Worth Metroplex

Pro-Motion Publishers

DEDICATION

This book is dedicated to all of the incredible professionals and companies who took the time to submit content to this book. It has been a pleasure working with each of you on the production of this book. The time you have all taken and the high-quality content that you have all shared has truly gone above and beyond anything we could have ever expected when we first set out to publish this book. Thank you to everyone who made this possible.

CONTENTS

Pro-Motion Publishers

ACKNOWLEDGMENTS

Professional Wedding Planning Advice has been made possible thanks to the following participants:

Rebecca Hackl Events/RHE Productions

Paper & Chocolate

LoveNotes - DFW Clergy Services

Shades of Sugar

A & L Floral Design

Dancemasters Studio

Hair Comes the Bride

The Beauti Studio

The City Club Dallas

Premier Transportation Services, LLC

Providence Place Bridal Boutique

Xquisite Events

Lone Star Travel

Hakim Sons Films

Jessica D'Onofrio Photography

INTRODUCTION

Thank you for purchasing Professional Wedding Planning Advice. When we set out to publish this book, it was our goal to obtain real world, usable advice from true industry experts. We are proud and excited to tell you that we have greatly exceeded even our own high expectations in this regard.

Professional Wedding Planning Advice is truly a compilation of the information that you absolutely must have before you embark on the massive task of planning your own wedding. Our interviewees have shared their knowledge and expertise to help your wedding go off without a hitch.

Very often in books that are written in this interview style, you'll find interviews with professionals who are mainly just interested in promoting their own companies. We are pleased to let you know that the contributors of this book have truly put your interests ahead of their own. As you'll see from reading these interviews, each of our contributors shares exactly what you need to do and what you need to avoid doing when you're planning your wedding.

Weddings can often be the subject of funny stories...for the guests. These same "funny stories," however, are usually nightmares for the bride and groom. In the great majority of cases, these unpleasant incidences could have been avoided if the bride and groom had just a little bit of "insider knowledge" when they were planning their wedding. The very nature of most weddings, however, is that it's a first-time (and often one-time) event where there are no second chances. The best strategy for getting it right the first time, therefore, is to learn from the experts, who have years of experience in the wedding industry.

After you read this book, you're going to have insights and knowledge that has taken years for our interviewees to acquire. Very often, married couples will look back on their wedding day, wishing they had done certain things differently. After reading this book, the likelihood of you having those same regrets will be greatly diminished. Your wedding is truly a milestone event in your life, and we set out to ensure that you get it right the first time—because hopefully, there won't be a second time! After reading this book, we genuinely believe that you will feel confident to plan your wedding with enthusiasm and certainty. So, without further ado, let's get into the interviews!

1 THE WEDDING PLANNER

When you are getting married, you have the option to plan your own wedding, or hire a professional. The biggest advantage of hiring a professional wedding planner maybe that it saves you a lot of time. In addition to that, dealing with all the different aspects of your wedding day yourself will bring along a lot of stress. Wedding planners are experienced in planning your wedding day, usually have good connections with all the vendors you need to deal with and can actually save you money in the process.

On the subject of wedding planning, we interviewed Rebecca Hackl from Rebecca Hackl Events/RHE Productions.

"For over fifteen years Rebecca Hackl has been envisioning, producing, and executing flawless events. As the founder of RHE Productions and Rebecca Hackl Events, she's been known for her extreme patience, calming nature, and close friendship with all of her clients, she will go the distance to provide premier service. Rebecca leads the team with a fresh approach and provides pioneering ideas that are unique to the event industry.

She has previously instructed at The University of Texas at Arlington teaching two certification courses - The Wedding and Event Planning Course and The Preston Bailey

Wedding and Event Design Course. She is a Certified Professional Wedding and Event Planning Instructor and a Certified Wedding and Event Design instructor.

As a mother of three teenage children, Rebecca loves to enjoy time with her family dining out and traveling, or just watching movies together on the couch! She gives her time to charitable organizations and currently acts event producer for The Leadership Gala, hosted by The Leadership Foundation. Rebecca sits on the board as President of the Ferrari Kid Foundation."

What are the main functions and responsibilities of a Wedding Planner?

What is a "Wedding Planner?" Two simple words, yet so much meaning and detail behind them! Ultimately, the main function of a Wedding Planner is to listen to the client's desires, translate that into a vision, and build the vision into their dream.

What are the advantages of hiring a Wedding Planner, as opposed to a couple planning their own wedding?

When a newly engaged couple begins their wedding planning process, there are hundreds of ideas, questions, and friendly advice being served upon them, and it can be extremely overwhelming! Even to the most experienced wedding pros, the role of a bride and groom takes on a whole new life of its own, and it can be complicated for most of us. The biggest advantage of hiring a professional Wedding Planner is not only to elevate the stresses of this process, but it can also save you thousands of dollars as a result of their experience and knowledge, as well as multiple hours you will save by hiring a planner. The fee for the planner more than pays for itself when your stress-free wedding dream comes true!

After hiring a Wedding Planner, can the couple, as well as friends and family, still help in planning the wedding?

There are numerous tasks that take place for the bride and groom during their wedding process, so help from family and friends should be happily welcomed, but also controlled. The couple's wedding should be their vision showcasing their style and personality; therefore, it's important to communicate your vision to your family and friends so that they can effectively help. Save the budget planning and vendor discussion to your planner; however, seek friends and family assistance with those tasks of finding the perfect pictures for your photo montage, researching the right bridesmaids' shoes, and selecting your wedding music. Couples, accept help, communicate clearly, and enjoy the attention!

Is it a good idea for a couple to hire a Wedding Planner if they don't like being told what to do?

There are many brides and/or grooms that prefer to be plan all the details of their wedding from beginning to end. There are various reasons why couples fall under the "do it yourself" title, and one of those reasons is because either one or both bride and groom prefers to have complete control. They feel like they have all the knowledge they need to plan their perfect wedding. In this case, a Wedding Planner may not be needed during the planning process, but may be preferred for their wedding day coordination. Not all planners are created equally, as we all have different styles and personalities.

What can a Wedding Planner offer that wedding planning books and wedding planning software cannot provide?

Wedding planning tools are literally at your fingertips with your online search. Very handy, but it can also be incredibly overwhelming. The planning process has evolved by leaps and bounds over the past decade, and I truly feel that my clients today come to me more confused than ever. A bride's style can change as quickly as her favorite blog is updated.

The difference between online tools and a professional Wedding Planner is that we have the ability to customize a wedding according to our client's style, personality, and budget. We have the experience to discuss the pros and cons of ideas and make the ideal suggestions for their perfect wedding. No book or software can compare.

If a couple is on a tight budget, can they afford a Wedding Planner?

Depending on your wedding details and budget, sometimes a Wedding Planner for your full planning needs may not be needed—or may not be an option. Sometimes the best money spent will be $200-$300 to sit with a planner on an hourly base to help get you started, point you in the right direction, and answer a few questions along the way. That money can save you hundreds of dollars, save you time, reduce your stress, and help guarantee that you've selected the perfect vendors and venue for your wedding! They can also give you creative ideas that can make your wedding unique on your budget.

How much money should a couple set aside for the services of a Wedding Planner?

Before seeking your partnered Wedding Planner, identify your needs and challenges in order to best select your level of planning service. Planners are available in all price, style, and personality ranges. Just like knowing what you want before shopping for a car, you must know what you want before shopping for your wedding. Most planners charge a flat fee for their services, but some will charge by percentage of your total wedding budget, or by the hour. After you've identified your total wedding budget, then it's helpful to know which level of compensation is right for you. For an experienced Wedding Planner, consider setting aside 15% of your total wedding budget for complete planning assistance.

What should a couple look for in a good Wedding Planner?

When researching your perfect Wedding Planner, look for years of experience and the number of weddings they've produced. While interviewing, find a planner that inquires about you and then listens to your story and ideas. Be careful of someone who dominates the conversation and challenges your ideas. Ideally, you want someone who compliments you both because you will be spending much time together throughout your planning process.

What should a couple look out for when selecting a Wedding Planner?

Be careful of a planner that talks too much about their life, tells you "no," insists that it must be their way, and is demanding of others, those are all red flags.

If a couple will be getting married in a location that is far away from where they live, should they hire a Wedding Planner that is close to where they live or close to where their wedding will be? Please explain why one of these options would be better than the other.

Planning a destination wedding, whether 300 miles away or 3000 miles away, can be truly exciting during the first stage, but after diving into the daunting process you may decide it's time to seek professional help. Hire a Wedding Planner? Yes. Next question: enlist in the service of a local planner or a planner within your chosen destination? I may have some planners oppose my answer to this, but based on my experience, I'm comfortable suggesting that couples contract a planner within the destination of their wedding.

This is because the planner is aware of their vendors and can plan according to their market. Here's my exception: If the wedding is located within another country, then I feel it's important to contract a local planner where you live and have her/him research your selected destination area. Often times your hired local planner will partner with a destination planner, and they will collaborate to ensure all your details are handled successfully.

You can contact Rebecca Hackl Events/RHE Productions here:

www.rebeccahacklevents.com
www.rhe-productions.com
rebecca@rhe-productions.com

2 HOW TO WRITE THE PERFECT WEDDING INVITATIONS

A wedding invitation is the first impression of your wedding day. There are so many choices these days that it can be overwhelming to pick the right one for you. Are you going to create them yourself or do you want to hire a professional to do the job? Whatever your choice is, after reading the interview with Vicki Petersen from Paper & Chocolate, we know you are well on your way to the perfect wedding invitations.

"Paper & Chocolate is a gift and stationery store located in Inwood Village. We work with brides to select and order their wedding invitations. Our many wedding album companies provide all types of printing: engraved, letterpress and thermography. We can design your custom invitation from a variety of papers, typestyles, colors and designs. We also work with our brides on their other wedding stationery, which can include programs, menus, hashtag signs, favor tags, place cards, table cards and thank you notes. We are also a lovely gift store with many ideas for hostess and special gifts.

We have a very large selection of unique greeting cards, fabulous chocolates, leather albums & accessories that can be personalized and a constantly changing array of special everyday luxuries."

How far in advance should a couple place an order for wedding invitations?

We generally suggest that once all the ceremony and reception information is finalized, it is a great time to start your invitation process. Wedding invitations should be mailed 6 to 8 weeks before the wedding date. This is the date you need to count back from allowing 6 to 8 weeks for proofing, printing, and delivery. Additional time may be required for your calligrapher, so you should contact whoever is addressing your invitations for their timing requirements. We also suggest planning the mailing of your invitations with holidays and special dates considered. For example, you don't want your wedding invitation to arrive in the midst of Christmas cards, as it may be overlooked, or on long vacation weekends like July Fourth. It may mean people are out of town so it might be stuck in the hold mail from the Post Office and just won't have the same impact. Don't forget, your wedding invitation is the first glimpse of your wedding, so you want it to definitely get noticed.

What is the standard way to make payments for personalized wedding invitations, with regard to deposits and paying the balance?

Once a stationery submits your invitation information to the printing company to obtain your first proof, there will be charges for your invitation. Most stationers require full payment up front, but some may require a 75% deposit with the remainder required when then invitations are picked up.

What measures can be taken to ensure that there aren't any spelling or other typographical errors on the wedding invitations before they are printed?

You should always request a proof of your invitation. The proof will not be an actual printed invitation because the plates for letterpress and engraving are not prepared until the proof is approved. The proof you receive will be a digital proof, often sent by email. It may not be the exact color of ink, but it will provide all the typestyles and format of the wording on your invitation. This proof should be very carefully checked to the point of spelling aloud each word to yourself as you review it to be sure you are noticing each detail. Check and double check all names, addresses and dates. Don't forget the standard "Who, What, Where and When" as it is possible to omit critical data.

Who actually mails the wedding invitations?

It doesn't matter who mails the invitations, but be sure it is someone you trust. The actual invitation and enclosures should be assembled and taken to the Post Office in exactly the manner your invitation will be mailed. This should be weighed by the Post Office in order to determine the correct postage required. Don't ever estimate the postage!

What should couples include inside of their wedding invitations?

The enclosures with the wedding invitation are optional.

The etiquette used to be that when someone received an invitation, they would write you a note to respond and let you know if they were attending. Now most couples provide a response card for the convenience of their guests. The response card requests the name of the guest, whether they are attending and the number attending. If there is a selection for dinner entrée, their selection is included with the response card. You can also include a separate reception card giving the details of the time and location. For special family members and guests, a small card indicating "Inside the Ribbon" may be included to direct them to their special seating for the ceremony. Maps showing the ceremony and reception locations may also be included with the invitation.

Who should the response card envelope be addressed to?

Most often the response card is addressed to the host of the wedding, which in most cases is the parents of the bride. There is no rule, however, so the response card can be addressed to the person who is keeping track of the information. This may be the bride or a relative.

What should an engaged couple be careful of when selecting a wedding invitation designer?

It is very important to select someone who is not only knowledgeable about stationery, paper, printing, etiquette and current trends but who also has long-standing, solid relationships with their wedding album companies. If something goes wrong, you need someone to stand behind you to be sure it gets corrected and you get exactly what you ordered and wanted. Paper is an essential part of an invitation. You select your invitation paper based upon color, feel, weight and size; therefore you should be able to see and feel the paper. Work with someone who understands what you want and has a commitment to quality and service as well as an excellent reputation in the community.

What are some of the advantages of hiring a professional wedding invitation designer as opposed to a couple creating their own invitations?

There are many aspects to a wedding invitation. As mentioned above, the paper, printing method and design make a first impression about your wedding. Unless you are a professional designer or very experienced crafter you may find creating your own invitation to be a challenge. We and our wedding album companies have specialized equipment for preparing your invitation. Special papers may be lovely to look at but may not take a standard glue to adhere to your layers. Envelopes only come in standard sizes from most of the commercial sources available to consumers. Wedding album companies produce envelopes to fit their special invitations in very large quantities. Then there is the etiquette and customs involved, which a stationery professional will know and convey.

What is the proper way to address a wedding invitation to a doctor?

There are many sources available to assist in all the variations for addressing envelopes to professionals. Crane provides much of this online as does the Emily Post Institute, and both companies have great etiquette books for reference. It depends on who is the doctor: If the husband is a doctor, it is addressed to Doctor (or Dr.) and Mrs. Smith; if the wife is a doctor, it is addressed to Dr. Mary Smith and Mr. John Smith. If both are doctors, it is addressed as The Doctors (Drs.) Smith, Drs. John and Mary Smith or Dr. John Smith and Dr. Mary Smith.

Should the names of deceased parents be included on a wedding invitation?

No, deceased parents should not be included on a wedding invitation. Parents' names are included in the invitation since they, as hosts, are "inviting" your guests to the wedding.

When a bride and groom are paying for most or all of the wedding, is it proper to put the parents' names on the wedding invitations? If so, how should the parents be listed?

If the couple is hosting the wedding they may select alternative wording. They may include their names at the top of the invitation, and they may "request the honour of your presence" (at a house of worship) or "request the pleasure of your company" indicating they are hosting the event. They may also include their parents' names in the invitation, but indicate in a separate reception card that they are hosting the reception by including your names at the top and "request the pleasure of your company" to your reception.

If wedding invitations are being sent to people who live at the same address, should one invitation be sent to each person or should one invitation be sent for everyone living at that location?

If you are inviting an unmarried couple living together the invitation should be addressed to them with both of their full names listed, and one invitation can then be sent to their address. If you are inviting roommates who are not in a relationship, then individual invitations should be sent. Each person in a household over the age of 18 and not in a relationship should receive their own invitation.

Paper & Chocolate can be contacted here:

5460 West Lovers Lane, Suite 236. Directly behind the Inwood Theatre Dallas, Texas 75209, 214-357-2739 www.paperandchocolate.com, info@paperandchocolate.com.

3 THE WEDDING OFFICIANT

Wedding officiants are obviously very important on your wedding day. They will lead your ceremony so it's very important to discuss that in great detail. In this interview you will learn about all the different aspects that come into play when hiring your wedding officiant. This interview was taken from Marty Younkin of Lovenotes ~DFW Clergy Services.

"LoveNotes~DFW Clergy Services is a highly respected organization of Dallas/Ft. Worth ministers and wedding officiants. It was founded in order to meet the needs of people who don't have a connection to a church or know a minister, priest, rabbi or judge, but need someone to preside over their special event. LoveNotes can provide ministers/officiants for weddings, vow renewals, baptisms, memorial services, christenings, baby namings, quinceañeras, house blessings, personal prayers, public invocations, and marriage coaching. All of the LoveNotes Officiants are licensed, ordained, experienced ministers who perform both religious and civil ceremonies. Our philosophy is "as you wish," so we have written a best-selling wedding book, A Wedding Ceremony To

Remember~Perfect Words for the Perfect Wedding, that allows couples to design their ceremony in order to have the wedding of their dreams."

How soon should couples book their date with a wedding officiant?

You can never book your officiant too early. He is the one person you must have. In fact, you only need 3 things for a wedding: the couple, the license and the officiant. If there is no officiant, there is no wedding, legally. But most brides want someone who not only will make their ceremony legal but also lovely. They want an officiant who "gets" them and understands their vision. If you wait until the last minute to secure your officiant, you might not have the kind of ceremony you always envisioned—one that fits you and tells your love story. Many officiants are booked a year or more in advance, especially during prime wedding months, so the sooner, the better.

What are customary policies regarding deposits?

Deposits are usually required to secure your date and time on the officiant's calendar. They vary from 30-50% down of your final fee with the balance due before the wedding date. Most deposits are non-refundable because the officiant turns down other weddings for your date and time and may not be able to book another wedding should you cancel. However, some officiants may refund a portion of your payment if you cancel well in advance, or if he is able to book another wedding in that time slot. Communicating with the officiant is always helpful, and exceptions to the rule are sometimes possible.

Is it typical for couples to meet with the wedding officiant prior to the wedding?

It is strictly up to the couple and their schedule. Some couples prefer to do everything online or by phone due to busy schedules and wait until the rehearsal or ceremony to meet their officiant. Others feel more comfortable meeting with their officiant beforehand so they can get to know each other and not feel like they are being married by a stranger. Personally, I feel that everything flows more smoothly when the officiant and the couple meet prior to the wedding so they can communicate feelings as well as words. It is important to make sure everyone is on the same page. Plus, the added benefit of building a relationship with the officiant always makes the ceremony seem more personal and warm, like he has been a family friend for years. This is the goal for a successful wedding ceremony.

If a bride and groom are of different faiths, or one of them is not religious, is that a problem?

That depends on each individual officiant/minister. Some ministers are bound by their denomination's rules, which may prevent them from being able to perform those types of weddings. Others, like LoveNotes, which is not connected to a particular denomination, have more freedom in marrying couples of different faiths or who are not religious. At LoveNotes, we believe the institution of marriage is ordained of God and that "all marriage should be honored by all men" (Hebrews 13:4). We wish to honor that by tying the knot for couples regardless of their cultural, religious or non-religious backgrounds. I would, however, encourage the couple to discuss these differences before entering into marriage to make sure this area won't be a source of conflict.

If the bride and/or the groom was married before, but is now legally divorced, will a wedding officiant marry them?

Generally, most wedding officiants will marry a couple if they are legally divorced, but some may ask to see the divorce decree. However, some denominations, such as the Catholic Church, are bound by certain rules they must follow, so the couple will have to go through the process of annulment before they can remarry.

Can children be incorporated into the vows?

"Family weddings" are very popular today. Whether you choose to include children by saying vows to them, presenting them with a gift or by participating in some family unity tradition together, it is important to make them feel like they are a part of this special day and this union. It gives them a sense of belonging. Sometimes, the bride and groom will say parental vows to the children and present them with a gift, such as the Family Medallion, as a keepsake for this special day when they officially became a family. Other options that incorporate children include the family unity candle, the blending of the sands, unity bouquet, and family knot tying ceremony. Children may also serve as part of the bridal party, ushers, guest book attendant, or as escorts for the bride and groom down the aisle. However you choose to include them in your ceremony, it is important that they are acknowledged in some way to make them feel as though they have a significant place in your new life. That being said, the challenge is to keep the focus primarily on the couple and not "the kids," as it is their wedding day.

Does the wedding officiant normally go to the rehearsal?

Well...how perfect does the bride want her ceremony to be? I cannot emphasize enough how important it is to have the officiant at the rehearsal, even if there is a wedding coordinator there. The coordinator and the officiant are each experts in their own fields. They draw on their own experience and expertise and work together as a team to make the ceremony flawless. The rehearsal is the time to work out any problems, make any changes and practice the ceremony mechanics so everyone knows who does what, when, where and how. The officiant, above all, needs to be aware of all these details since he is the one who conducts the wedding service. He is the "master of ceremonies." If he is not at the rehearsal and changes are made without being communicated, well... guess what happens? Since the ceremony sets the stage for the rest of the celebration, being well prepared allows the officiant to get things started out right.

How long does the wedding officiant normally stay after the ceremony?

Usually, the officiant will stay for photos and then leave. Oftentimes, he has another wedding or other commitment he must get to so he has to leave immediately after photos are taken with him. Most good photographers know to take the photo with the officiant first so he can leave quickly for his next appointment. If a couple wishes to have the officiant stay for the reception to offer a prayer before the meal, a fee is sometimes incurred to remunerate his additional time.

Does the wedding officiant wear a traditional robe or do they dress in other attire?

Unless the officiant's religious affiliation requires him to wear specific clothing, it is usually the choice of the bride and groom as to what the officiant wears. That choice depends on the mood they wish to set for their ceremony and how they want the officiant to look in their photos. Some of the attire choices may include a suit, tuxedo, robe with cross, robe without cross, western clothing or other costume that coordinates with the theme of their wedding.

How many couples can a wedding officiant marry at one time?

Each state has different requirements. In Texas, there is no limit to the number of couples an officiant can marry at one time. For example, the Ballpark in Arlington hosted a "mass wedding ceremony" on one special day for couples who wanted to get married there. As long as each couple has their valid marriage license to present to the officiant, they are all eligible to be married on the same date and at the same time by the same officiant.

How much are couples typically allowed to customize the ceremony?

Each officiant will have their own guidelines concerning the ceremony. Some will allow only the vows to be customized, while others give the bride and groom a free hand in creating the entire ceremony. At LoveNotes, we provide a ceremony manual that allows the couple to design their complete ceremony from entrance to exit. They may choose from a variety of wedding vows, ring exchange vows, readings, prayers and blessings, traditions and other special touches, along with diagrams for entrance, exit and altar formations. The good thing about a couple creating their own complete ceremony is that there are no surprises because they know exactly what the officiant is going to say at their wedding.

Do wedding officiants allow couples to write their own vows?

Most non-denominational officiants will allow couples to write their own vows. In fact, often it is encouraged to create something that comes from your heart because it makes your vows more personal. After all, these are promises for a lifetime. However, some ministers are restricted by their church's guidelines, which only allow certain vows. Many officiants will ask to preview them to ensure they are appropriate in nature for the wedding ceremony. This does not mean they can't be humorous in places nor personal. It simply means the vows should reflect the sincerity of the heart and the respectful nature of making a promise.

Will wedding officiants generally marry couples that are not members of a religious congregation?

Again, it depends on the individual officiant's religious affiliation and their guidelines. Most non-denominational officiants will marry couples who do not belong to a church or other religious congregation. Therefore, it is not necessary to secure a judge or JP to perform your ceremony. Yes, ministers are ordained of God to perform religious ceremonies, **but** they also are licensed by the state to perform civil or non-religious ceremonies if they choose to do so–as LoveNotes does.

Are friends allowed to participate in the ceremony, including giving readings, singing, or anything else? How should these things be coordinated with the wedding officiant?

Most all officiants/ministers will allow the participation of friends and family in the ceremony. They recognize that this makes the couple's ceremony more personal. It is crucial, however, that any details regarding participation of others in the ceremony be communicated to the officiant so he can include those in his ceremony notes. This is another reason why the officiant should attend the rehearsal, so all those participating can practice and the officiant is aware of the placement of the reading, prayer or song by the friend or family member. It would be a shame to mistakenly omit these details and run the risk of offending or hurting someone's feelings who was asked to participate and then forgotten.

How much do wedding officiants usually charge for services?

The fee depends on the level of services chosen by the bride. The average fee for a wedding officiant in the DFW metroplex is $200-$600. Some officiants may charge additional fees for specific ceremony options, rehearsals, consultation time spent with each couple, trip fees, time and day of week selected, size of wedding, venue, etc., while other officiants' fees are all inclusive (like LoveNotes). Remember, the officiant sets the tone for the ceremony, and the ceremony sets the tone for the rest of the celebration. So choose an officiant who will set the stage for the wedding day festivities and get the celebration kicked off on the right foot. When choosing a wedding officiant, the bride and groom should practice the 3 R's: Research, Reviews, Recommendations. The right wedding officiant is worth his weight in gold!

You may contact LoveNotes–DFW Clergy Services, here:

Marty Younkin
Executive Director
LoveNotes - DFW Clergy Services
www.lovenotesweddings.com
www.lovenoteslane.com
817-917-5540

4 THE WEDDING BAKERY

Ordering your wedding cake may seem straightforward but there are many factors that you should take into consideration. How big should the cake be, what flavors should be used, which colors and can you taste a sample before you order your whole cake? Learn more about ordering your wedding cake from Autumn Surface of Shades of Sugar.

"Shades of Sugar is a small bakery located just outside of Dallas in Richardson, TX. They customize in anything sweet and have a wide variety of confections available to order online and in the shop. The bakery is owned by Scott Brum and Autumn Surface. Scott bought an existing bakery for Autumn as a birthday gift, so she could fulfill her dream of baking. She has an excellent staff who decorates and helps create the wonderful sweets. At Shades of Sugar they aim to please with everything they create and serve."

How long before the big day should a wedding cake be ordered?

We have people come by and order two weeks before and some a year or more in advance. Depending on how big a role the cake plays in your dream wedding, that's when you should order. If your cake will be plain and is not the centerpiece that you are planning everything else around, then you should find the other important things like theme, color, design; that way the cake will fit with your other decor on your big day. Saving the date is the most important piece and some bakeries will let you put down a deposit to save the date a year or more in advance and then come back to actually make major decisions about the cake. I like to know the specifics at no less than 3 months in advance just so I can plan around that. It is better to know what theme you want, what colors you want and have a good design in mind when you come into the bakery, because there are so many choices that it can be overwhelming to make those decisions on the spot.

What are some factors that determine the various prices of wedding cakes?

The price at my bakery is determined by the size and design of the cake. The more intricate the design, the more time it takes to pipe. Fondant and gum paste also take time and are more expensive so they in turn cost more.

What are some of the different ingredient and flavor options that can be selected for wedding cakes?

If you can dream it up, we can try to make it. We aim to please our customers, so we will try to make the type of cake that is most pleasing to them.

Do wedding cake bakers generally allow couples to sample cakes before ordering them? If yes, is there usually a cost for this?

We do free cake tasting and design. We know we have a delicious product so we will let you taste it for free, because I know you will come back to order.

Can special instructions/arrangements usually be made to account for people with certain food allergies?

Yes, we will make every effort to accommodate allergies. This usually carries some extra cost, but as always we aim to please. Some options could be to include a gluten-free, sugar-free, etc. satellite cake if you know there are people attending who would need this.

If there are pre-arranged flowers that need to be placed on a cake, who normally does this?

We prefer to let the florist handle fresh flowers. I think that each person has their own look. If all the other flowers are done with a certain look, then the cake may stand out if someone else does it. I tell my brides that if they are already paying a florist then let them go ahead and do it. I will add fresh flowers to a cake if the customer wants that, but I work with their florist to ensure the flowers are the same quality and color. If they do not have a florist, then I work with a local florist to provide the best flowers possible to make the cake beautiful.

Do wedding cakes usually include a cake topper, or is this ordered separately?

Toppers are ordered separately by the couple. I can order it, but most of the time they have something in mind already and there are so many places online to get them, it is just as easy for them to order it themselves. I do give them the necessary information to order the right size and have them bring it in to ensure that the look is what they want.

Who normally puts the cake topper on a wedding cake and when is this done?

We will set up the whole cake including the topper. There is a setup fee, but as long as it is arranged at the time of the order or before final payment then we provide that service.

What if more people will be attending the wedding than were originally expected? What can be done to ensure that there will be enough cake for these extra guests?

We offer several options. We can add satellite cakes or even sheet cakes to be served from behind the scenes. We can do petit fours to help make up the difference. Sometimes we get creative and add cookies, cupcakes, or cake balls to match the cake.

Who is normally responsible for delivering the cake to the reception location?

We can do the delivery. There is a fee for that service. If the customer picks up the cake, then we cannot take responsibility for anything that may happen during transportation. So we do recommend that the bakery delivery to the location.

Is a delivery charge standard on wedding cake orders?

Yes, we charge a fee depending on miles from the bakery.

Shades of Sugar can be found at :

581W Campbell Rd Ste 121 Richardson, TX 75080, 972-235-2253, www.shadesofsugarbakery.com.

5 THE WEDDING FLOWERS

You can make your wedding day perfect with the right set of flower arrangements. Make sure you pick a florist that has done weddings before and has photos to show you of all the different weddings that where done. Most florist will advise you on the subject of colors and sorts of flowers that can be used. Some flowers are harder to get in specific seasons and that can add up to the price tag. Make sure they have access to your wedding/party locations as they will need to be there in advance. Read all about wedding flowers in this interview with Lauren Schick and Amanda Chorn, owners of A & L Floral Design.

"A & L Floral Design is an independent, family-owned Dallas-based wedding florist that specializes in creating unique wedding flowers and designs for weddings and events at a reasonable price. The women of A & L Floral Design are passionate about offering full-service wedding designs and custom arrangements, and provide delivery services within the DFW metroplex. They strive to create the most beautiful bouquets and memorable arrangements, tailoring each design to your specific needs and tastes. There is no greater satisfaction than making someone smile

— a fulfilling experience that they are blessed with on a daily basis."

What should couples be aware of when selecting a florist for their big day?

Before hiring a wedding florist, it is important to get to know his/her own personal style and design philosophy. Like many elements in weddings, florists can create and or tailor arrangements to your specification. It is also helpful to find out if the florist has any ideas for your wedding. Discuss your theme and colors. Discuss your tastes and your vision. Also, make sure the florist can help you choose flowers that will help set the intended mood during the wedding.

Finally, it is important to verify how many other events the florist will do on the same weekend and who will be delivering the arrangements to your wedding venue. Find out if the florist will set up your arrangements or leave that up to the venue manager and his staff.

What are some simple things that a couple can do to ensure that their flowers are consistent with what they visualized for their wedding?

Even if you are unfamiliar with specific flowers, you can still choose the color of the flowers to match your wedding. The florist will be able to help you figure out which flowers are best to match your color needs. In addition to helping you choose color, a professional florist will know which flowers will be available during the month of your wedding. Spring and summer weddings will have a different selection of flowers available than fall and winter weddings. Out-of-season flowers may still be available, but you may have to pay a premium to get them brought in from elsewhere and you risk high quality of the blooms. Make your designer aware of the type of arrangements you prefer. Also discuss the flowers you dislike.

Be prepared to discuss your specific flower needs when you meet with the florist. Will you decorate the church or just the reception venue? Where will the flowers be placed within each location? Who will be wearing flowers during your event?

Can wedding bouquets be customized, or can only certain flowers be used in bouquets?
Every single arrangement for a wedding is 100% customizable to fit into the bride's vision!

What is the customary process for placing deposits and paying the remaining balance?
Most wedding florists require a deposit to reserve the wedding date, and then the remaining balance would be due a couple weeks to a month before the wedding. Our company requires a 25% deposit, which is non refundable and is required to reserve a date on our calendar. We then require the remaining balance to be paid a month before the wedding, to ensure adequate time to preorder all required flowers for the wedding.

What is the difference between a ladies' buttonhole and a corsage?
A ladies' buttonhole (also referred to as a pin-on corsage) is similar to a men's boutonniere, but normally includes more blooms (two or more) along with ribbon accents. A women's corsage is worn similar to a bracelet on the wrist and includes numerous blooms (three of more) and includes ribbon accents.

Are the flowers for the ceremony and the wedding reception two separate orders, or are they typically all ordered as one package?

The entire wedding is normally ordered in one package. To ensure a consistent look throughout the entire wedding (ceremony and receptions), it is important to have the same florist provide all of the arrangements. If multiple different florists are utilized for the wedding, you may have end up having flowers that don't match (different shades of the same color, etc.).

How far in advance should couples order their wedding flowers?

Florists will typically only do 2 or 3 weddings in one weekend, so the earlier you reserve a florist the better to ensure availability. Before meeting with a florist, it is important for couples to have their venue reserved, color scheme picked out, and an idea of the guest count.

Considering that weddings take place on specific times and dates, how can a couple ensure that wedding flowers are delivered at the right time for the ceremony and the reception?

A florist can estimate the amount of time that delivery and set up will take, and therefore once a florist knows the start time for the ceremony and reception, the florist can help guide the couple on the appropriate delivery time. Additionally, couples should ensure that the agreed-upon time is included in the florist's contract.

Is it fairly common for couples to meet with the florist prior to their wedding? If so, what should a couple bring with them to a consultation?

It is very common and very important for a couple to meet with a florist before their wedding. During a consultation, florists will talk through each and every possible item that a couple may be interested in for their wedding. It is very helpful for the couple to come to a consultation prepared with pictures and ideas of arrangements. Also, it is helpful when couples share their floral budget with the florist, so that the florist can guide the couple on what is feasible within their budget.

Approximately how much should a couple budget for their flowers in proportion to their entire wedding budget?
If a couple is interested in flowers for both their ceremony and their reception, then they should budget about 10% of their overall wedding budget for flowers.

Is it true that flower prices fluctuate throughout the year? If so, by how much do these prices fluctuate?
Flower prices fluctuate greatly throughout the year. Most flowers can be found year round, but their price while in season can be as much as 5 times less than when they are out of season. Additionally, flower prices will increase across the board around certain holidays such as Mother's Day, Christmas, etc.

To get in contact with A & L Floral Design, give them a call at either (214) 762-3035 or (214) 762-3200 or send them an email at aandlfloraldesign@gmail.com. Additionally, feel free to find them on the web via their website at www.aandlfloraldesign.com, on Facebook at www.facebook.com/AandLFloralDesign, or onTheKnot.com

6 THE FIRST DANCE AT YOUR WEDDING

The first dance on your wedding should be a couples perfect romantic moment. Even if you danced together before, the wedding dance still is something special. When you start to practice as early as 6 months in advance, with the help of a dance instructor, you have all the time of the world to make the first dance your best one ever. Learn everything about the first dance at your wedding from Nancy Henrichsen of Dancemasters Studio.

"Dancemasters Studio has been teaching Dallas to dance socially and competitively since 1984 in all styles of partner dancing from beginner to advanced levels. Our studio is known as the friendliest ballroom dance school in the Dallas area, and our students love the warm atmosphere from the first moment they enter our front door. We offer a full schedule of classes every week with a variety of different styles of partner dancing, as well as private instruction for students wanting more individual attention. Our weekly Friday night parties with recorded music provide a beautiful smoke-free nightclub environment for social dancing on the best ballroom dance floor in the area, and

feature a 16-piece big band orchestra once a month for your dancing pleasure."

What should an engaged couple bring to their dance lessons?

If they have selected their music for their first dance at their wedding, they should bring it with them to their first lesson as well as any ideas they would like to share with their instructor about their dreams for their first dance. Many couples bring a video sample of something they have seen that they would like to incorporate into their dance, which is very helpful. Otherwise, just bring a positive and open mind about preparing for their big day.

Why should an engaged couple take dance lessons prior to their wedding?

The first wedding dance is a special moment that both celebrates their marriage and symbolizes their partnership as a couple. It is the first dance together as man and wife, and will be forever a beautiful memory and a highlight of their wedding reception. To fully enjoy their spotlight moment, preparation well in advance of their wedding day will ensure that the couple can enjoy their first dance to the fullest, as well as enjoy social dancing to many styles of music.

Should the engaged couple already have their wedding song picked out prior to their lessons?

Yes, if possible, it is ideal to have music selected so that the instructor can focus on teaching the appropriate style of dance that will fit their special song. Having their song picked out will also maximize and utilize lesson time to the fullest potential. However, if the couple has not picked out their song upon arrival at their first lesson, the instructor will be available to assist them and possibly make some recommendations.

How long should the couple's main wedding dance last (i.e. the couple's first dance)?

Two minutes is appropriate unless the couple has previous dance experience and has the ability to perform an entertaining routine that will keep everyone's attention for a little longer. Even if the couple can perform an exciting routine, it should be kept to under 3 minutes. 3 minutes is a very long time when you are dancing or watching a solo.

What are some of the most appropriate dance styles for the couple's main wedding dance?

We typically use waltz, rumba, fox trot, or nightclub 2-step because these dances most frequently fit the style of music most couples select. Because most couples choose a song that has special meaning to them, their music may not fit the usual style of dances used, so it isn't uncommon to incorporate East Coast Swing or Salsa into the routine.

How many lessons should an engaged couple typically take, so that they are prepared for the big day, and what will they learn at these lessons?

It will depend on the couple's dance goals and their ability as to how many lessons they will need. If the couple has simple aspirations for a basic fox trot, for example, they can probably have a respectable outcome with 10-20 lessons. However, if a couple wants a more complicated choreographed routine, they will need more lessons, depending on their dance ability.

Do the bride-to-be and groom-to-be both need to attend the dance lessons at the same time? If not, how do ballroom dance instructors typically work around situations where both people can't be present for their lessons at the same time?

It is best to take the lessons together as a couple to learn how to partner as a couple. However, in the situation where both the bride-to-be and groom-to-be are not able to attend at the same time, instructors will work with each of them individually and still achieve a nice result.

What are some of the main differences between group and private lessons? What are the advantages and disadvantages to each?

Group classes are taken in a group setting with other individuals or couples, ranging from 5-20 or more people. Private lessons are in a setting with one instructor per student or couple. Obviously, students receive one-on-one instruction in private lessons, whereas there is little one-on-one instruction in a group class setting. Private lessons are more time efficient because instruction is focused on the individual or a couple's unique needs and desires. More can be accomplished with individual instruction than in group settings. Group classes are usually much lower in cost that private lessons.

Group classes frequently rotate partners, giving everyone a chance to dance with both beginners and more advanced dancers, helping both the student's lead and follow, and there is an opportunity to form strong friendships in a group class setting.

Should the couple wear any specific types of shoes to their lessons?

Dance shoes are not required, but are certainly helpful to allow the proper foot movement across the floor. Rubber soles stick to the floor and can contribute to knee and ankle injuries, and do not allow any gliding of the feet. Smooth leather soles can be slippery on the dance floor and also be a risk factor for injuries. It is helpful if the bride-to-be can practice in the shoes she will dance in at the reception.

What is the best way for a couple to select a wedding dance studio and/or an instructor?

Referrals are always the best way, but if not available, couples should look for a studio that is conveniently located and accessible from work or home. The studio website is often a great way to learn about the available instructors and the professionalism and atmosphere of the studio itself. Calling different studios and talking to the receptionist can be helpful as well. If the receptionist is warm and welcoming, then it is likely that studio will have a welcoming environment, and will be a happy place to receive instruction.

Does the couple typically bring their own music to each lesson?

Only if they want to dance to the music they choose or if they will be dancing to a particular song. Otherwise, most competent studios have a beautiful variety of music appropriate for almost any style of dance.

What if the bride-to-be or the groom-to-be is far more experienced in dance than their partner? Is it still possible (and advisable) to take lessons together?

Of course! All the better! If one partner has more experience, it can actually work to their advantage. There may be some catching up to do by the less experienced partner, and that partner may choose to take some individual lessons to help them with their particular needs. But overall, they can totally take effective lessons together.

What types of clothing should students wear to their dance lessons?

Casual clothing is appropriate, but some studios prefer no jeans or shorts. Something casual yet comfortable, such as slacks or skirts for the ladies, and slacks and casual shirt for the gentlemen is appropriate.

How far in advance should a couple start taking dance lessons before the big day?

Many couples are surprised that they cannot learn to dance in one or two lessons. How many lessons are needed will depend on the couple's goals and dance experience. We usually recommend 4-6 months prior to the wedding so that they will feel comfortable in their first dance as well as in other styles of partner dancing.

Is a wedding dance usually a choreographed/pre-planned routine?

Many couples choose to have their first dance choreographed and begin working on it several months in advance. These days it has become more and more in vogue to perform a lovely first dance at the reception. But it certainly can be a less formal routine based on a few simple steps and patterns which can be learned in 10-20 lessons.

You can contact Dancemasters Studio in the following ways:

Our website: www.dancemastersdallas.com
Studio address: 10675 E. Northwest Highway, Suite 2600B
Dallas, TX 75238
Phone: 214-553-5188
Email: contact@dancemastersdallas.com

7 THE WEDDING HAIRSTYLIST

Do you already know what hairstyle you want on your wedding day? There are lots of options and because of that it's important to think about this early. It may be necessary to start working on your hair days or even weeks before the wedding to get a perfect end result. For this chapter we interviewed Gina Ludwig from Hair Comes the Bride.

"Hair Comes the Bride was started in 1996 out of a love and passion for bridal beauty. In the 17 years since the business was started, it has grown to include service areas across the United States. Every year, Hair Comes the Bride helps thousands of brides and their friends and family to look and feel their most beautiful by providing on-location bridal hair and makeup services. Hair Comes the Bride also offers a huge selection of designer bridal hair accessories and wedding jewelry through their online boutique. Hair Comes the Bride's philosophy is that every bride deserves to look and feel her most beautiful on her wedding day and shouldn't worry about what anyone else thinks. She should stay true to her own unique style and create a wedding day look that truly represents her personality and makes her feel uniquely beautiful."

Can a bride-to-be usually schedule a consultation session prior to her "big day" appointment?

It is not usually necessary for a bride to schedule a consultation session prior to her trial run appointment. The consultation is typically something that will be done during her trial run. However, a stylist may want to do a phone consultation or do what we do at Hair Comes the Bride, which is to send the bride a consultation questionnaire for her to fill out before her trial run. The questionnaire is something that helps us to get to know her needs and wants a little better and tells us a little bit more about her personal style and the style of her wedding so that we can be prepared for her trial run appointment and ensure that it runs smoothly.

How far in advance should a bride-to-be book her appointment?

It is always best to secure your wedding date with your bridal beauty company as soon as possible so that you do not run the risk of the company you want being booked with another wedding. I would say that most brides book their bridal beauty services approximately 6 months before their wedding date. However, this does not mean that you need to do your trial run appointment six months in advance. First, get your wedding date secured with your bridal beauty company, and then as your date gets closer have them contact you to book your trial run appointment. We recommend that a bride book her trial run appointment somewhere between 6 to 8 weeks before the wedding date. This is close enough to her wedding date that her hair length and color will be the same or very close to what it will be on the wedding date.

It is also far enough from her wedding day that worst-case scenario, if she is not happy for some reason with the trial run appointment, she still has time to make other arrangements. Keep in mind that if you go with a bridal beauty company who has several stylists, if you are not happy for any reason it is very likely that the company will have another stylist that they can book you with for another trial run appointment. And, in some cases, as it is at Hair Comes the Bride, they may even be willing to do another trial run for free. If you book your bridal hair and makeup with an independent solo artist and you're not happy with your trial appointment, you have to start all over again looking for another stylist.

Should a bride-to-be always have a "trial" session, so that she can see what her hair will look like before her wedding? Are there situations where a trial would not be needed?

It is highly recommended that the bride always have a trial run session before her wedding day. The bride is the most important aspect of the wedding day. Above all else, the flowers, the cake, the location, all eyes are on her! Therefore, in my opinion, it is important that the bride not take any chances with her wedding day look before her big day. I know that some brides may be tempted to try to save money by forgoing the trial run appointment, but honestly, booking the wrong stylist can really make or break the start of your wedding day. Your stylist is a literally the vendor who is with you, by your side right before you walk down the aisle. You need to make sure that your stylists is not only able to create a wedding day look that you love and truly represents your personal style and the style of your wedding, but you also need to make sure that your stylist is punctual, professional, and calms you down on your wedding day as opposed to stressing you out!

The only way you're going to really know these things for sure and have peace of mind is to meet and work with your stylist at a trial run appointment. Now, all of that being said there certainly may be situations where a trial run is not feasible. This is usually going to be the case with an out-of-town or destination wedding. If you are planning an out-of-town or destination wedding and there is absolutely no way you will be able to meet with your stylist before your big day, it is just that much more important that you do your research and pick a stylist or bridal beauty company that is trustworthy and that you feel confident in. Also make sure that they are willing to do a phone or even a Skype consultation with you before the wedding day and finally make sure that you have a fairly good idea of what type of hair and makeup style you're going to want on your wedding day. Another option for your hair and makeup for your out of town or destination wedding is to have a trial run with a local bridal stylist and have her take detailed notes and several photographs of your hair and makeup so that you can take them with you and present them to your stylists on your wedding day.

How does a trial typically work?

The trial run appointment is going to be the time in which you and your wedding day stylist will want to determine and finalize your bridal hair and makeup. The trial run typically starts with a sit -own consultation between the bride and the stylist. This is an opportunity for your stylist to get to know you better and to find out more about your personal style and the style of your wedding. There are many factors that go into helping to determine the best hair and makeup options for a bride, including such things as the bride's hair (length and thickness), the bride's coloring, her dress, her wedding day colors, her flowers, the location of the wedding (will it be inside, outside, hot, cold, etc.), the style or theme of her wedding and then of course also her likes and dislikes and her every day personal style. And, these are just to name a few. It is important that a bride finds a stylist who is willing to educate her and help her choose a style that is right for her as opposed to dictating to her what she "should" or "shouldn't" do. A stylist shouldn't be afraid to give her opinion about what hair and makeup she thinks will be best for the bride, but she should also remember that it is just that, her opinion, and that ultimately it should be all about what makes the bride happy and makes her feel beautiful. Once the stylist has asked the right questions and helped the bride to determine what will most likely be the best wedding day style for her, it is then typically time to actually style the hair and makeup so that the bride can see exactly what she will look like on the wedding day. Once the stylist is done styling the bride's hair and makeup, it is then typically time for the bride and stylists to go over the look and make any changes if needed. My biggest piece of advice for brides regarding the trial run appointment is, speak up! Don't be afraid of hurting your stylist's feelings. If they are a true professional, they will understand that hair and makeup is subjective and if you don't like something it's not a personal reflection on them.

A bridal stylist's goal at the preview appointment should be to make you happy, no matter what it takes. If for any reason you feel as though your stylist is not respecting you or is making you feel bad in any way at the trial run appointment, I highly recommend that you look for another stylist. It is just not worth the risk of having him or her affect you negatively in any way on your wedding day. Finally, the trial run is typically also going to be the time in which your stylist is going to want to have you sign a contract and finalize the details of your wedding day such as, what time you need to be finished and how many services you will need to have done.

How long does a bride-to-be's hair need to be in order for her to wear it up?

If a bride can get her hair into any type of a ponytail (even a small one), then she should be able to wear her hair up. A talented bridal stylist is going to have techniques that they can use to get short hair into an updo. Although, keep in mind that the longer and or thicker a bride's hair is the more options she is going to have when it comes to putting her hair up. If the bride is willing to use hairpieces and/or hair extensions, then she is going to widen her range of options considerably. Again, make sure that you find a stylist who is experienced in styling shorter hair and is also comfortable using hairpieces and/or hair extensions. With the right hairpieces and/or extensions, the sky really is the limit when it comes to wearing your hair up.

What types of accessories can be used in a wedding hairstyle?

Brides have more options than ever when it comes to what type of accessories can be used in a wedding hairstyle. When Hair Comes the Bride first started over 17 years ago majority of brides were wearing a classic bridal tiara. And while the tiara will never go out of style, more brides nowadays are leaning towards a more understated hair accessory including bridal combs, bridal hair pins or bridal hair flowers. Another hair accessory that has gained popularity in the last few years is the headband. A bridal headband can be worn traditionally behind the ears and across the top of the head for a more classic timeless look or can also be worn across the forehead for a whimsical, Bohemian look.

Should a bride-to-be wash her hair before arriving for her appointment?

I don't think that a bride needs to worry about washing her hair before her trial run appointment. Her stylist should be able to work with her hair in whatever way she shows up for her appointment, whether her hair is clean or dirty. Now, for the wedding day, this may be a different story. A bride's wedding day hairstyle is going to need to stay for several hours so it is important that her hair be prepared properly. But, this is really going to depend on the bride's hair type and the style in which she is going to be wearing her hair. For instance if a bride has very dry hair she may not want to wash it before the wedding day. If on the other hand a bride hair tends to get oily very easily she is going to probably want to start out as clean as possible and have her stylist "dirty" her hair up using product. This is something that your stylist should go over with you at your trial run appointment.

What should a bride do if it rains on her wedding day, if it's windy, or if there are other forms of bad weather?

I think the only thing a bride can do regarding bad or extreme weather and her bridal hairdo is to number one, be aware of what possible conditions she may encounter and number two, be as prepared as possible for such conditions. For instance, if a bride is getting married on the beach, it is very likely that she may encounter some windy beach weather so this is one of the factors that she is going to want to take into consideration when deciding what hairstyle is going to be best for her, and she is going to want to be as prepared as possible for dealing with the windy weather. One of my favorite things to recommend to a bride who is getting married outdoors and may encounter windy weather and who is planning on wearing a veil is to invest in a set of veil weights to hold her veil down when the wind blows. Same thing goes for extreme cold weather, extreme hot weather, rain, snow.

The only thing a bride can do is to try to be as prepared as possible. If there's even a slight chance that it may rain, invest in a nice, big golf umbrella. If it's supposed to be a hot sunny day, make sure that you have a good touch-up powder in case you start to sweat your makeup off. Maybe invest in a little battery-powered fan and, again, make sure you have a nice big umbrella to shade you from the sun.

Should a bride-to-be take anything into consideration with regard to the hairstyle she selects for different times of year/different seasons?
There are many things that a bride-to-be should take into consideration when deciding on what hairstyle is right for her, and the time of year is certainly one of these things. More than anything else (and as I mentioned before), the weather during any particular time of year should certainly be taken into consideration when deciding on the right hairstyle. The fact that your wedding is in the middle of August and the weather is typically in the 90s or above during this time of year, I would imagine is going to be taken into consideration when deciding whether to wear your hair up or down, for instance. Besides the weather, however, I don't think that the time of year or season is really that important in determining your style, especially compared to other factors such as your personal style, your hair type or the style of your wedding. I think that a beautiful updo, a half up half down style or an all down bridal hairstyle can certainly go with any season.

What should a bride-to-be do for her hair in the days and weeks leading up to her wedding?

In the days and weeks leading up to her wedding a bride should do what she can to make sure that her hair looks its absolute best on her wedding day. She will want to make sure that even if she is growing her hair out to wear a certain style on her wedding day that she continues to regularly get her hair trimmed to cut off any dead split ends. She will also want to make sure that if she colors her hair it is done anywhere between two and five days before her wedding day so that the color is fresh and looks its best. If a bride typically colors her hair on a regular basis she is going to know on which day her hair color usually looks its best after having it done. The weeks and days before your wedding is not the time to try something new, including a new style, a new color, or a new hairstylist. A bride may also want to consider doing a nice deep conditioning treatment on her hair a few days before the wedding day. She can have this professionally done, or there are plenty of wonderful over-the-counter deep conditioning products to choose from.

You can contact Hair Comes the Bride in any of the following ways:

www.haircomesthebride.com
1-800-485-4444
info@haircomesthebride.com

8 THE MAKEUP ARTIST

In addition to a hairstylist, most couples also hire a makeup artist. It's important to discuss how you want to look in advance and make sure you hire a makeup artist who has experience with bridal makeup. A professional makeup artist will make sure you look your best but not overdone. For more insights into the makeup part of the wedding day, we interviewed Kristin Colaneri from The Beauti Studio.

"Kristin is a native of Dallas, but lived and worked in NY for six years. She has experience in runway, print, theatrical, headshots/modeling, and bridal. At the Beauti Studio, we would love to take care of all your beauty needs: makeup, hairstyling, private beauty lessons, makeup classes, brow grooming and airbrush tanning!"

Does the entire bridal party normally use the services of the makeup artist too?
Yes, that´s very common.

How long does the whole process take?

It depends on size of party but usually no more than 5 hours.

Is it best for the bride-to-be to have her hair done first, before the makeup, or the other way around?

I usually 'set the hair' before the makeup, then style her hair last.

How do makeup artists work with clients who have sensitive skin and various skin types?

Well, we make sure to have a variety of products in our kit that work with several different skin types. Using mineral makeup and skincare that is good for sensitive skin is best.

Will makeup typically be used that has been used on other clients? What sanitary factors should a bride-to-be ask about when speaking with makeup artists?

Yes, the same makeup is used; however, the brushes are cleaned properly with each use, and there is no double dipping into products that are creams, like mascara, etc. Also I spray my products with alcohol. Brides can ask about this for sure. She really should be working with a professional makeup artist that has trained and has a lengthy resume such as mine.

What is airbrush makeup?

It's micronized foundation that sprays through an airbrush gun. It is water-resistant and feels like cool air on the face. It is best used in HD filming.

Is it a good idea for a bride to wear lashes on her special day if she's not used to them? Why or why not?

Yes, they look fantastic and really give added glamour! If a bride has never worn them, I will usually put on individual lashes. If the bride has a very thick lash line base, then it isn't necessary to do them; like I said, they just look great!

What are the best types of makeup products for a bride to wear on the big day?

She should wear professional products that are long lasting. There are plenty of makeup lines that are really great, like Makeup Forever, or MAC, or Laura Mercier, but I also have my own makeup line at the studio.

When a bride uses a makeup artist, will she look too "overdone"?

No, not at all, but it depends on the artist. I make sure the foundation always looks like skin.

How does a makeup artist ensure that the bride looks good on her big day, both in person, and in photos too?

Airbrush is the best. It covers really well without looking cakey. During the trial run, we take pictures in the studio to ensure how it will photograph. I do not let the bride leave dissatisfied.

What factors and options usually determine how much a makeup artist charges?

Level of education and experience. I should charge more based on that; however since the economy hasn't been great, I have to also set pricing up based on the going rate in a particular market.

Do most makeup artists do pre-wedding consultations with the bride-to-be and the wedding party? Is so, what is typically discussed at a consultation?

Yes, we do a consultation/trial run with the bride prior to the wedding. We discuss bridal style and looks for the day. Then we run through them so the bride knows what to expect.

Should the bride-to-be and the bridal party hire the makeup artist for a trial run first?

Yes, but only the bride really needs it. If anyone else would like it, then they are welcome to book a trial run, but it is not necessary.

How far in advance should a bride-to-be book a makeup artist?

She should book it about 6 months in advance.

Does the makeup artist typically come to the bride-to-be, or does the bride-to-be travel to the makeup artist?

I usually go to the bride; however, I have a beautiful studio that they are always welcome to book at.

Does the bride-to-be usually need to have special equipment such as special chairs, lighting, or mirrors for the makeup artist?

No, a good makeup artist brings everything they need.

You can contact the Beauti Studio in any of the following ways:

469.560.0132
5612 SMU Blvd. #205 Dallas, Texas.
www.beautistudio.com

9 THE WEDDING VENUE

If you are looking for a wedding venue for your reception or ceremony, there are a lot of things to take into consideration. Each venue has different services and accommodations. What do they provide you and what should you arrange yourself? If you hired a wedding planner there is a good chance they know more about the wedding venues in your area and what they have to offer. For the following information about wedding venues we interviewed Vicki Welch of The City Club Dallas.

"Originally founded in 1918, The City Club is one of the original and most prestigious private clubs in the City. Upon arrival into the Dallas area, one is immediately welcomed into the city with the view of our unmistakable downtown sky-line, complete with the green-lit accent of the Bank of America Plaza. Located high atop this building, the tallest downtown, The City Club offers the most spectacular view of the city, as well as countless, highly recognized entertainment venues and historical landmarks. Inside, well-appointed quarters and beautiful décor provide the perfect setting for private parties, seated

dinners, or unforgettable receptions. The entire club can accommodate up to 500 guests for receptions, or 300 for seated dinners. The City Club invites you and your guests to experience the breathtaking panoramic views as well as be pampered by our first-class staff and cuisine.
The City Club is also available for special events:

- *Wedding Ceremonies and Receptions*
- *Corporate Meetings and Receptions*
- *Rehearsal Dinners*
- *Seminars*
- *Private Parties*
- *Private Meeting & Dining Events*

The City Club strives to provide added value to our members and guests by maintaining a distinctively high level of quality in our services and cuisine. We custom tailor our services to address each member and/or guest's special needs."

For how long/how many hours should a couple book a venue for a wedding reception?
The standard time is 4 – 5 hours. Most receptions are 4 hours of event time. Occasionally, if a couple would like a separate cocktail hour, the time requested will be 5 hours. Of course, the length of time may vary depending on the religion and traditional cultural requirements.

If a wedding reception runs longer than the number of hours it was booked for, are there overtime charges?
Yes, most venues charge a per hour fee for every hour over the contracted amount. At The City Club, the charges is $350.00 per hour over 4 hours.

How should a couple decide which type of room to book for their wedding?

Couples should choose the type of room based on capacity first. Will the room accommodate their number of expected guests? Additionally, the shape and décor of the room is very important. Is there anything to distinguish the room from other rooms and venues? Couples should also feel comfortable with the coordinator and/or Wedding Consultant at the venue.

What are some of the fees typically associated with booking a venue?

The following are a list of fees that are charged by the majority of venues. (The City Club does not charge for those in bold.)

- The main two fees are the room rental and food/beverage minimum requirements.
- Attendant fees
- Bartender fees: total evening or **by the hour**
- **Regular staff fees**
- **Cake cutting fee**
- **Security fee**
- **Parking fee**
- **Cake stands**
- **Easels**
- **Rental of china, glassware and silverware**
- **Rental of tables and chairs**
- **Rental of linens**
- Charge for going over the estimated time
- **Charge for coordinator/ Wedding Consultant**

What is generally included in the rental of a room?
Usually it's the house tables (guest and display), chairs, linens, china, silver and glassware and basic décor.

Is it customary for catering halls to provide tables, chairs, linens, china and silver? If yes, are there usually additional fees for this?
Many places, including City Club, do provide. A lot of places do not and require the client to rent them.

Do prices for catering halls generally vary by day of the week or the time of the day that the event takes place? If so, how and when do prices fluctuate?
Yes, many venues are priced higher on weekends in the evenings. The City Club allows for discounts during the week to include Friday and Saturday AM if the club is already booked in the evening for a wedding.

Do catering halls generally require couples to use a specific caterer, or can the couple bring in an outside caterer?
Catering halls will allow outside catering. Most venues, like Private Member Clubs or restaurants, will require that you use the in-house catering.

How does it typically work with liquor, beer, wine, and champagne? Is this usually furnished by the catering hall, or does the couple have to provide this?
If the venue has a Texas Liquor License, outside alcohol is not permitted per TABC. If the venue does not, the client is usually welcome to bring in outside liquor.

If a couple would like to have a microphone available for speeches, is this generally provided?

Most venues required that the couple use the DJ or band mic for speeches. The City Club does allow the use of a complimentary mic for speeches only.

How does it work with insurance for the event, and what types of insurance are customary?

Most venues require that the vendors provide proof of liability insurance. Some require that the bride and groom also provide insurance. The City Club has only the vendors provide proof of liability insurance.

What is the customary deposit to leave prior to the event?

The deposit varies with each venue. Hotels usually require a higher deposit. The City Club only requires the room rental plus 1/3 of the food/beverage minimum.

If the event is cancelled or re-scheduled, is the deposit refundable?

The deposit is normally not refunded. At The City Club it is definitely not refunded, as the space was being held and we turned away other business.

If the event is being held outdoors, are tents normally provided? If so, is there an additional cost for this?

There is usually a cost for tent rental. You will want to contact Ducky Bobs for pricing.

With outdoor events, if the weather is very bad, how does a venue typically accommodate for these situations?

Some venues provide alternate locations, but some do not.

Are there usually additional fees for cleanup? If so, how is this typically calculated?
Most venues charge and additional fee for cleanup. The City Club does not unless something like confetti is thrown on the floor.

Are tips/gratuities standard for catering hall staff? If so, what is the customary gratuity that should be left?
Most tips/gratuities should be covered by the gratuity charged by the venue to the client. However, often if the client feels they have received extraordinary service from one or more of the staff or the Wedding Planner, they will offer an additional tip.

You can contact The City Club Dallas in any of the following ways:

The City Club Dallas
901 Main Street
6900 Bank of America Plaza
Dallas, TX 75202
214-748-9525
vwelch@cityclubdallas.com
www.cityclubdallas.com

10 THE WEDDING LIMOUSINE

If you want to use a limousine as a means of transportation on your wedding day, you are sure to make a memorable entrance and exit. Most limousine rental companies have a small fleet of different limousines to choose from, all for different budgets. You have the option to use them for a part of the wedding day or all day long when needed. Some couples even take their families along to enjoy the ride. To learn more about booking a wedding limousine, we interviewed Laurie Johnson from Premier Transportation Services, LLC.

"Founded in 1996, Premier Transportation in Dallas, Texas offers an extensive fleet of late-model vehicles including limousines, limo buses, vans, SUVs, shuttle buses and coach buses. Choose Premier for an airport transfer for one, wedding transportation for 2 or 200, shuttle buses for a corporate event, or a stretch limousine for a night on the town.

Premier has been named Best Wedding Transportation for three years in a row by the American Association of Certified Wedding Planners. Premier was also recently named the National Operator of the Year by our industry association and trade magazine. We have won numerous other national and local awards and honors, including an A+ rating (the highest ranking) from the Better Business Bureau.

Our experienced staff and highly professional chauffeurs are committed to providing safe, reliable transportation, exceptional customer service, and consistent and equitable pricing.

Our office is open twenty-four hours a day, seven days a week, three hundred and sixty-five days a year. We provide in-house dispatchers who support our clients and chauffeurs at all hours of the day or night.

Our wide variety of luxury, chauffeur-driven vehicles can accommodate from one to 56 passengers, in the Dallas-Fort Worth Metroplex and all over the world with our Global Affiliate Network.

You name the occasion – we'll make the ride flawless. Whether you require a chauffeured vehicle for business or pleasure, close to home or in a new city, Premier Transportation is always there. Our goal is to make your travels safe, effortless and on schedule."

What should a couple's budget be for wedding limousines?

A wedding limousine is a very personal choice, depending on the formality of the wedding, the overall budget, and the personal style of the couple. Some couples just want a basic sedan for a quick getaway, while others require a stretch limo or specialty car that they will use for the entire event. For a simple getaway, the total price can range from $175.00

to $650.00. For a limo that will be used for several hours, prices will start around $500.00 and go up from there. The savvy wedding couple should shop around and compare pricing and vehicle options with several transportation vendors. (NOTE: The prices listed above are only examples for transportation based in the Dallas-Fort Worth area. There is not a standard limousine price, and pricing will vary among different vendors and different areas of the country.)

In addition to the wedding limousine, the wedding client should also assess other transportation needs including: shuttle buses for the guests, party buses for the bachelor/bachelorette party, sedans for family members, transportation to and from the airport for out of town guests, etc.

How far in advance should a couple book the limousines for their wedding?

The transportation industry in Dallas runs in cycles – hectic in the spring and the fall, and less busy in midwinter and during the summer. If the wedding occurs from March through June, or in October-November, the limousine should be booked at least three months in advance. For weddings that occur in the slower seasons, it's still a good idea to book at least a month in advance. Advance planning and early vehicle booking is the best way to assure that the wedding client gets the preferred vehicle at the best price.

Approximately how many people can fit in one limousine?

There are several sizes of limousine – usually ranging from 4 to 10 passengers. Some specialty limousines, like stretch Hummers, may accommodate up to 20. Another popular vehicle for a wedding is a standard sedan, which can hold a maximum of 4 passengers.

It's not unusual for a wedding party to exceed 20 people, and then the wedding client needs to consider a bus option. Buses can come in a variety of sizes and styles – from 14 to 56 passengers, and in standard or limo-style seating. These vehicles are very popular with wedding clients, and often take the place of a limousine.

Do limousine rental prices vary, based on when the actual wedding takes place? If so, how does this work?

As noted earlier, there are several months during the year that are busiest for transportation companies. During those busy months, prices and hourly minimums can vary. Many specialty vehicles like limousines require a 4-hour minimum for regular weekends. During the busy season, that hourly minimum may increase to 6 or 8 hours. In addition, some companies may also raise their hourly rates during the busy months. In general, transportation companies are locally owned and operated, and each one may have a different pricing structure. This is another reason why it's important for the wedding client to shop around and compare pricing, vehicle options, and company reliability.

Do couples typically pay for the limousine while it's waiting?

A limousine service typically stays onsite throughout a wedding event – for example, taking the passengers from hotel to church to reception and back to hotel. The hourly rate for the limousine is charged throughout that time, even while it's waiting with no passengers. The client needs to understand that, even when the vehicle is idle, the transportation company still has to pay the salary of the chauffeur, plus all the operating expenses for the vehicle – gas, insurance, etc. Plus, time waiting for one client means that the vehicle can't be used by any other clients.

In addition, it's in the client's best interest to have the vehicle waiting on standby, and being paid for that time. There may be guests at the wedding who need to leave early – due to age, illness, etc. The vehicle is completely at the client's disposal throughout the reservation time, so it can make multiple trips to accommodate unexpected emergencies or other special requests.

Can limousines be rented for short periods of time, such as for one hour?

In some cases, a transportation company will offer a wedding transfer rate, for example, for a quick trip from the reception to the hotel for the wedding couple. But the more common practice is to require an hourly minimum, often about 4 hours. There are a number of reasons for this. First, the vehicle is very expensive to purchase, insure, operate, and maintain. Second, federal regulations require that the chauffeur be paid a minimum number of hours, regardless of the trip time. Third, it's not practical for a limousine company to take a one-hour reservation, because that will prevent them from taking a longer reservation from another client. Many wedding clients request a one-hour transfer at the end of the evening, just to take them from the reception to their hotel. They need to understand that they will usually be required to pay for the hourly minimum, even for this short trip. It's usually not possible for a transportation provider to cover their costs with a one-hour limousine reservation.

What types of limousines are most popular for weddings?

Every wedding is different, as is every wedding budget. Luckily, there are several different styles of vehicles and prices that can accommodate the variety of wedding transportation requests. The most popular vehicles are the standard stretch limousine and the specialty car, like a vintage Rolls or Bentley. Some wedding clients are looking for exotic transportation, like a trolley or a stretch Hummer. And some couples just want a basic sedan or SUV for a more casual event.

Plus, most weddings require additional vehicles for guests and larger groups. Shuttle buses are extremely popular with wedding clients, as they can transport large numbers of people more safely and efficiently than individual cars.

Can the wedding party bring alcohol into the limousine?

Chauffeured vehicles can accommodate any food and beverages, including alcohol. Many transportation companies stock the vehicle with glassware and napkins, and some even provide water and ice at no additional charge. Wedding clients are welcome to bring champagne or any other drinks aboard the vehicle.

If a wedding needs to be cancelled or re-scheduled, how do most limousine companies handle this?

Because each transportation company is probably an independent vendor, there is not a universal cancellation policy. Plus, during the busy months discussed above, the cancellation policy may vary. In many cases, the client may cancel up to 48 hours prior to the event with no penalty. However, during a busy month like April, the client may be required to prepay the entire amount, with no refunds in the event of cancellation. Again, this is why the client needs to shop around and gather information about the cancellation policy before choosing a transportation vendor.

In most cases, the client can reschedule to another date with no penalty, as long as there is sufficient notice. However, a reschedule during the busy season could still result in extra charges like those described above. This is another question to ask when the client is comparing vendors.

Are there any other fees typically associated with limousine rentals? If there are, please explain these fees.

Most transportation companies have a pricing structure that is multi-tiered. First is the base rate, which covers the basic vehicle operation. Then there are administrative fees, which cover office staff, building and office equipment overhead. Next is a fuel surcharge, which covers the additional cost of higher gas prices not included in the base rate. Finally, many companies include a standard gratuity for the chauffeur in their prices. If all of these costs are provided in the initial quote, this is called the all-inclusive rate. Wedding clients need to be aware that each transportation vendor will have its own way of quoting prices – some only quote the base rate, some quote base rate plus fees only, etc. But the client will still be expected to pay the base rate, plus the fees, plus the fuel surcharge, plus the gratuity. The client needs to be sure when comparing prices that they are getting the all-inclusive rate from each vendor.

Is smoking normally allowed in limousines?

Most transportation vendors do not allow smoking in any of their vehicles. It is nearly impossible – plus very expensive – to remove the odor. The vendor would run the risk of offending a lot of other customers with the smell, so it's much more practical for the business to maintain all vehicles as smoke-free.

If the wedding runs longer than expected, who is responsible for the extra time?

Every vehicle is reserved for a set amount of time. However, transportation vendors know from experience that a trip may run longer than originally scheduled. Of course, the extra time must be charged for, and the original client is responsible to pay the additional cost. Some clients make a reservation for a minimum 4-hour block, and stipulate that the vehicle leave promptly when that time is used. They need to be aware that this may leave the chauffeur in a very awkward position, as it is his job and his training to accommodate the passengers in their requests. It would be best for the wedding client to employ a Wedding Planner or other designated person to coordinate the transportation, especially if there are time constraints or other special requests around the transportation.

After the deposit is paid, when is the balance normally due?

Because each transportation vendor does business differently, the deposit and payment structure can vary. The time of the year may also impact the requirements for deposits, prepayments, etc. During the busy season, a deposit up to 100% may be required to book the reservation, and then any balance is charged prior to the event. In other cases, or during the slower months, a smaller deposit may be charged at the time of booking, and then the balance is charged after the trip is done. Some companies don't require a deposit at all, depending on the event and vehicle type. For the final payment, some companies charge the entire cost up front, and some companies charge the full amount after the completion of the trip. This is another question that the wedding client needs to ask when shopping for a transportation vendor.

You can contact Premier Transportation Services, LLC in any of the following ways:

Premier Transportation Services
1341 W Mockingbird Ln #201W
Dallas, TX 75247
Phone: 214-351-7000
Email: reservations@premierofdallas.com
Website: www.premierofdallas.com

11 THE BRIDAL SALON

When you are planning to go to a bridal salon, make sure you call them for an appointment. Most bridal salons work that way so they can take their time with you. It's also good to ask if you can bring friends along and if you should bring anything with you. Picking the right wedding dress that you feel comfortable in is very important, make sure you take your time. For this chapter we interviewed Lynette Coughlin from Providence Place Bridal Boutique.

"Come see us at Providence Place Bridal, your one-stop wedding shop! Here at Providence Place, we are known for our amazing price point and superior customer service. We provide bridal gowns by Maggie Sottero, Mori Lee, & Casablanca. We also carry dresses for bridesmaids, mother of the brides/grooms, flower girl dresses and bridal accessories. We have tuxedo rentals as well through Jim's Formal Wear."

If a bride-to-be sees a gown online or in a magazine, can bridal salons typically get specific brands or styles that they don't usually carry?
Salons can only order from brands they carry in their shop because they have an account with those specific brands. As for styles, usually salons can order a style from the brand they carry, even if they don't have that specific style as a sample in their store. However, it is always best to ask the salon first because some brands have separate divisions within their bridal lines so that may limit salons on ordering specific styles.

What is the price range for a bridal gown and what determines this price range?
Bridal gown prices can greatly vary. However, the average bride is willing to spend around $1,000 on her bridal gown. Bridal gown prices vary depending on designer, material, and the vendor's cost for each gown.

How does the process work for ordering a dress and having it ready in time for the big day?
Most designers will provide their vendors with an estimated production time for their gowns so they can inform brides what the approximate time would be for ordering. On average, most brides should allow about 6 months for ordering; this does not include alterations needed after the dress comes in. Bridal gowns are usually made small, so when a bride is ready to order she will be sized according to the specific designer's measurement chart. From their the designer will order the correct size and color wanted and will be given an approximate delivery time for the dress. From there the vendor will keep the bride up to date on the status of her dress and delivery time.

What are the dress sizes that are available for bridal gowns?

On average, most designers have sizes available from 2-28. Keep in mind these sizes are usually not equivalent to everyday sizes; they are made small. Brides usually have to order a size or 2 bigger than what they would purchase in their regular clothing.

How does a bride-to-be determine which dress size to order?

Sizes are determined by consulting the designer's measurement chart. Most bridal salons will take bust, waist, and hip measurements to determine the bride's size in the specific designer. If the gown can be ordered a custom cut to fit, then other additional measurements would be taken to order the dress specifically to the bride's dimensions. Every designer is different in regards to either having set sizes to order or making their gowns custom to order.

Why would a bride-to-be need to order extra fabric, and why is this sometimes requested?

Extra fabric is usually ordered when a bride is making changes to her dress with alterations; i.e. making straps, making sleeves, adding a corset back, taking a corset back out, etc.

Do bridal gowns come in petite sizes? If so, what are the sizes in this category?

Most designers will offer different gown lengths for petite size brides, but they are technically not true petite sizes with a shorter torso length. Not all dresses or designers offer gown-length options.

What is a "hollow-to-hem" measurement?

The hollow to hem measurement measures from the soft, where your neck connects with your collar bone, down to the desired hem. This helps in determining gown length.

Do bridal gowns only come in white? If not, what are some other colors that a bridal gown can come in, and when would a color other than white be appropriate?

Most gowns can be ordered in white or ivory. Designers are now offering other color options such as blush, gold and champagne. White is very traditional, but we are finding more brides are wanting their gowns in ivory because it is a softer color and most people can't tell the dress is not white when the bride is wearing it. Majority of brides are breaking tradition and color does not matter to them.

Why would a bride custom order a gown as compared to purchasing one that is already in the store?

Most of the gowns in stores are samples that have been tried on before. Brides want their own gown straight from the designer that other girls have not tried on. It is kind of a special bond with the bride and her dress, the one only she has tried on.

What is a "trunk show"?

A trunk show allows salons to showcase styles from the designers that they may not have in their store on a regular basis. Majority of trunk shows will also offer special pricing on the dresses featured in the trunk show.

What is a blusher? Is this something that brides still wear?

A blusher is the top layer of the veil which pulls over the front of the bride's face. Most brides opt to not have a blusher. Only brides requiring a blusher for religious or traditional reason wear them.

Do veils have to be ordered separately, or are they included with the gown?

Veils are ordered separately usually through their own designer.

What is a bustle?

A bustle is the term applied to pulling up the train. Usually a seamstress will apply little hooks or ties to pull the train up on the dress and make it all one length for the reception.

How do brides store their gowns before and after the wedding?

Before the wedding, gowns are usually kept in plastic hanging bags provided by salons. After the wedding, brides will either put the gowns bag in the hanging bag or pay to have their gown preserved.

What should a bride-to-be bring to the alteration fitting?

For a fitting, brides should bring the proper under garments they are going to wear under their dress as well as the shoes they are going to wear on their wedding day.

What is the customary deposit needed for ordering a gown?

Most salons will require anywhere from 50-75% of the total gown amount for a deposit to order.

Should a bride-to-be call in advance to schedule an appointment if they are coming in for a fitting?

Most salons require a scheduled appointment in order to try on dresses. Some places may be a little more relaxed with walk-ins, but you should just call ahead and schedule an appointment so you are guaranteed the opportunity to try on gowns and a sales associate to help you.

You can contact Providence Place Bridal Shop in any of the following ways:

Providence Place Bridal Shop is located at 2065 Summer Lee Dr. Suite 101 Rockwall, TX 75032. The shop is open Tuesdays through Saturdays 11-6 and Sundays 1-5. We are closed on Mondays. Our phone number is 214-435-8962 and our email is proviplace@gmail.com. For more information please refer to our website www.purelyprovidential.com

12 THE WEDDING PARTY RENTAL

Most items that you need for your wedding day party can be rented. A lot of rental companies have special items for weddings. If you hired a wedding planner they have probably used a wedding party rental before and can give you some good advice. Be sure to ask your rental company about items that are often forgotten for a wedding, they have experience in this field and are more than happy to share it with you. For this chapter we interviewed Bhavna Dharni from Xquisite Events.

"Xquisite Events is a boutique rental company capable of intimate or large scale productions. We specialize in lighting, and dance floors but also carry audio, video, drapery, chiavari chairs, and much more. We offer a turnkey production service for our clients from conception to execution. With a strong focus on customer service, we have quickly gained a reputation for quality and excellence in our market."

How do party rental companies ensure that equipment is only provided at the exact time of the ceremony and/or reception?

We have a checklist system that is triple checked. The checklist includes not only the individual items needed but also load-in time and event start times, so you can have the full picture to make the best decisions regarding logistics. All the details must be known to allow for the smoothest process.

Do party rental companies usually have a minimum order size for delivery?

Some companies in the industry do. At times it does not make business sense to entertain a small client and use valuable company resources (time and energy). Most the vendors we know do not have a minimum.

What if a couple needs more equipment after a delivery has already been made?

Any good rental company would do everything in their power to make the couple happy, especially if it is feasible. When it comes to our clients, we strive to make the impossible possible. However some factors do play a part in having to say no, time usually being the main factor.

What should a couple do if they did not receive all of the equipment they ordered, or if they are not happy with the condition of the equipment?

You should reach back to your point of contact at the company and ask for a refund. Depending on the many variables, the rental company should give back a partial refund or full refund. To minimize these issues, do your homework. Meet the company. Hopefully you know someone who has used them before; you have to trust the company you are going to use for your event!

What if a couple needs to contact their party rental company in an emergency, after normal business hours?

When you decide on your rental company, your sales person should give you their cell number. We provide our clients with our cell numbers to reach us after hours. Please make sure it is a true emergency and not an overreaction to a small issue. You do not want to abuse this service. We prefer clients call us immediately with any emergency so we are up-to-date, always.

Who typically sets up the equipment?

A professional should always be setting up the equipment. To ensure it is done properly for your event and for future events, the equipment is always handled by trained personnel!

What should be done with dishware, flatware and glassware before it is returned?

All glassware should not have liquid in it. Flatware should be in its proper container, and dishware should be free of large particles of food. Your CC is held on file for damaged, lost or broken items.

What do you suggest a couple does if they need to keep equipment longer than originally planned?

The client must let the rental company know as soon as the need arises. Additional costs may apply. Logistically the rental company would need to adjust strike and load-out times and allocate resources properly.

How can couples typically see the equipment they're think about renting ahead of time?

The couples have a couple of ways to see the equipment. One, you go to an event where the company is providing the equipment you are using, and you can get a first-hand look at an actual event. Or you may ask to go to their warehouse and see the items you will be renting. They all will have samples, and many will show you the exact product you will be renting.

Do party rental companies usually deliver the equipment, or is it normally picked up?
Only a trained qualified individual handles the equipment. If it is something simple as table linens, etc., we do allow for customer pickup.

With regard to having equipment available for weddings that are during off-hours, how is that normally handled?
Rental companies do add an off-hours surcharge for labor and delivery to accommodate the special needs of wedding clients.

Do party rental companies typically do deliveries and/or pickups on Sundays or holidays?
Yes, they do; however there is an extra charge for the holiday and Sunday pickup. It is best to coordinate with your venue and rental company and keep a good open line of communication to ensure everyone is on the same page.

You can contact Xquisite Events in the following ways:

Xquisite Events
5139 Sharp St. Dallas, TX, 75247
Office: 214-233-5097
Website: www.xerentals.com
Facebook:www.facebook.com/xerentals
Instagram: http://instagram.com/xerentals

13 BOOKING YOUR HONEYMOON

Your honeymoon should be relaxed and romantic. Destinations can vary, from cruises in the Caribbean to a romantic hotel in Paris, we all have different ideas about the perfect honeymoon. Travel agents can give you good advice and often have years of experience when it comes to honeymoons in all of the different destinations. For advice about booking your perfect honeymoon, we interviewed Donna Alkarmi from Lone Star Travel.

"I have over 16 years of experience as a travel agent and 4 years working for the airlines. I have travelled to the far East, Middle East and all over Europe in addition to MANY trips to Mexico and the Caribbean to make sure I keep up on current trends and resort conditions. My best line of defense is knowing the key staff members at many of the resorts I deal with so IF there is an issue, I know who to call to get it remedied quickly. I never charge fees and offer payment plans. My prices are normally less or the same as those .com companies, but you get me, available 7 days a week to be of assistance to you. My clients are all over the US since I plan many destination weddings and honeymoons in addition to my regular clients."

Where are the most popular honeymoon destinations?

Based on the couples' budget and best bang for the buck, the Mayan Riviera of Mexico, mainly because of the wonderful, romantic, adult-only, all-inclusive resorts this area has to offer. If they have a larger budget, Tahiti is always a favorite place to just relax and enjoy the South Pacific. They also have to have much more time to take on Tahiti or Fiji because of the time it takes to get there, which is about 10 hours from Dallas, not including connection times on the West coast.

What is the average price of a honeymoon?

For Mexico, total for 2 persons, 5 nights $3500.00 for a 5-star, adult-only, all-inclusive resort on the beach, which includes nonstop airfare and nonstop transfers to the hotel. Of course, high season or holiday travel would be more expensive. Nice thing for my clients is that the deposit would only be $50.00 or $150.00 per person (depending on airfare), and final payment is not due till 45 days prior to departure so they can budget their money. I also offer a honeymoon registry for my couples in case they have enough pots and pans and prefer their guests to give towards their honeymoon, whether it be the actual trip or a possible swim with the dolphins experience or a couples massage. For Tahiti it would be closer to $8000.000 - $12,000.00 depending on the accommodations. Since all brides want that over-water bungalow, it does come with a price tag!

Can a couple be married at their honeymoon destination? How does this get arranged?

They can, but some countries are easier than others. I don't recommend they get legally married in any country. Go to a

JP here first, then do a symbolic there, with the looks and sounds just like a wedding with the beautiful backdrop and pictures to last a lifetime. Not only is it less stressful with some countries requiring blood to be drawn for tests, documents to be translated and a trip to the city court house, but also less expensive that way. Also, what a lot of couples don't realize is sometimes it takes 3-6 months to receive your marriage license in the mail from these destinations, which could delay couples from getting new licenses, getting on the spouses insurance plans, etc... I plan many destination weddings and mainly use the onsite wedding coordinators to assist my brides while I deal with all the guests flying in from all over the US. I also get a promo code so all guests get a discount on the price; in return my couples get perks from the hotel for getting married at the resort. I always connect the wedding coordinator to the bride initially, and then the two of them will iron out the details.

How do cruise and land resort honeymoons differ?

Personally, I don't recommend a Caribbean cruise for a honeymoon. It's not that romantic since kids are running around and too impersonal. A lot of first-time cruisers do not know that tips, alcohol or soft drinks are not included in the typical Caribbean cruise. Now, if they have a healthy budget, then a European river cruise may be a great way to see many areas of Europe. You unpack once but experience up to three countries in one swoop. Most river cruises are geared towards adults, with smaller ships to fit in the rivers rather than the oceans, which also allows you closer proximity to the city centers. Wine and beer and soft drinks are normally included in most river cruises. Some even include the gratuities, and all offer tours free of charge in each port. All-inclusive resort honeymoons are really the way to go. The price you pay will include everything from room service, tips, alcohol, soft drinks and all the food. Most of the resorts I use for honeymooners also have a Jacuzzi for 2 in the room to add to the romance factor. There is nothing like sitting on your balcony watching the tide come in or the sun setting.

Should a couple specify that they are booking a honeymoon while making reservations? Is yes, why?

I always ask anyway; that way I can make sure the resort is geared towards honeymooners and not a swingers' resort! I also notify the resort or hotel to make sure they get a king bed (although always a request, I've not had one problem to date on getting it!). Some resorts offer honeymoon or anniversary amenities as well, like discounts on couples massages, fruit and champagne in the room, breakfast in bed to drawing a two-person Jacuzzi bath in their room complete with champagne, bubbles and rose petals.

What are some unusual and unique honeymoon destinations?

Gorilla trekking in Africa. Also fantastic wildlife safaris, boat cruise, cultural tours, adventurous mountain hiking, chimpanzee treks, and excellent bird watching among other services.

How should a couple prepare so that their trip goes well?

Talk to their trusted travel agent, and make sure they are personally familiar with the area about which you are inquiring. Having someone who has been there will make your trip go well. I give insider advice on what to expect or hold your hand during the booking process and make sure you feel very comfortable before you leave. I use dedicated tour operators that specialize in different areas around the world that I have access to in case something goes wrong.

Don't trust your honeymoon to an online booking engine, because they offer zero support and most likely if you need help, you could get someone on the phone that does not care or has no experience in the country you are in and can't give solid advice. A good travel agent will be available to you while you are on your trip. I give my cell # to all my clients and tell them to text or call me if they need me, anytime. The biggest piece of advice when choosing a travel agent is to have them interview you both to make sure they are matching you with your dream getaway and not a package the agent is benefitting from. No two couples are the same, and no travel agent should be forcing you to go somewhere you don't feel comfortable.

What is an "adventure honeymoon package"?

Costa Rica is an adventure destination for couples. This is for those wanting to zip line in the rain forest, see howler monkeys and other forest creatures on the way to their boutique hotel overlooking the active Arenal Volcano while watching the lava glow at night from their room. Relax in the hot springs with breathtaking waterfalls. It is an oasis of calm and an ecotourism heaven. Whether you are looking for a city full of nightlife, adventure in the jungle or relaxation on the beaches, you can find it on a tour like this. You've also got whitewater rafting; hiking; sky trek; canopy tours; coffee tours; and boat tours to watch whales, dolphins and turtles.

What should a couple bring with them on a honeymoon cruise?

If it is just a Caribbean cruise, just an original state-certified birth certificate and a government-issued ID like your license, but passports are recommended. And bring lots of money for the extras not included in the base cruise price (as mentioned above).

What are some of the best vacation destinations for honeymooners?

I think anywhere in the Caribbean or the Mayan Riviera of Mexico that can offer you a romantic resort with a great beach are great choices. Activities like canoeing, zip lining, and snorkeling are always fun for couples, or if you are interested in history, some cultural excursions to learn about the Mayan Aztecans can be fun and educational. Again, this question is best answered after interviewing the couple; then I can make recommendations based on the conversation. After a hectic wedding, most couples do not want to take a 10-12 hour flight to arrive at their destination; that is why the Caribbean or Mexico is a favorite getaway from Dallas and most East coast cities. Most flights are 2 ½ - 4 hours long so you are there in a relatively quick period of time.

What does the term "destination wedding" actually mean?

It's a wedding or ceremony where you travel to a vacation-like setting, normally a beach outside the US or Hawaii where family and friends attend. It's not to be confused with an elopement.

How does a couple plan for their honeymoon?

Make an appointment with an experienced travel agent and bring all your wants and desires to the meeting. Looking online can be deceiving. Just talk to each other and decide what you both want, and your travel agent should be able to match you both to that perfect getaway based on your budget and time restraints. Please have a budget in mind when you meet with your agent; this greatly helps us target in on a good match for you both.

How far in advance should a couple book their honeymoon?

6-8 months would be a good gauge. But if you are taking a honeymoon over a holiday like New Year's or Spring Break, then 9-10 months is preferred. Keep in mind, airfare is not loaded in the system till 10 months prior to departure. I have couples always wanting a rough idea. I don't mind doing that, but I can't guarantee that will be the price when you decide to book. And prices on air and sales on resorts change on a daily basis, so the early bird gets the worm.

What should a couple look for in a travel agent?

Ask, "Have you personally been there? How long have you been a travel agent? Do you charge fees?" A lot of agents now charge fees, and you should be aware of this before you engage. I personally do not charge fees, but that is just me! A good agent will not only price one company, but many to get not only the best pricing, but as many amenities as possible for your honeymoon. Not all travel agents are romance agents. Get the right agent for your special getaway. Just like a doctor, we all specialize.

What are the standard/customary tips and gratuities that are paid on a honeymoon?

If it is an all-inclusive, then none except the driver that takes you from the airport to your hotel. If you find you really like this particular bartender or waiter at your all-inclusive resort and you want to give them a tip, then $2.00 is equivalent to a $6.00 tip in the US. If you are not at an all-inclusive resort, it depends on the country and star quality of the resort you are staying. A lot of restaurants now include the gratuities in other countries, so read your bill carefully.

Lone Star Travel can be contacted at:
www.Lonestar-Travel.com or 972-658-6351.

14 THE WEDDING FILMMAKER

Filming your wedding day or parts of it can make you relive your wedding day for years to come. As counts for most of the other areas, choose an experienced filmmaker who can show his previous work to you. Filming a wedding day is a field apart. This chapter will give you some great insights about wedding videography. We interviewed Derek Hubbard from Hakim Sons Films.

"Cinematic masterpieces are what we construct. Telling your story while capturing all the fine details and illuminating your wedding experiences for generations to come is what we do. Our business is a family tradition that stems back three generations: from a grandfather who sought vision and innovation to a grandson who excels at it. Today, the Hakim Sons family has grown into a team of dedicated and passionate cinematographers and creative artists who make it their mission to use their talents to tell your unique story. Our films transport you to your special day again and again as you see, hear and feel one of the most important days of your life. It's priceless, sentimental and very personal. It's a document of life."

What are some of the options and features that a couple should consider for their wedding video?

Your wedding is the most important day of your life, and you want to make sure your story is documented in a way that is tailored to your style. Whether that means capturing sweeping, Hollywood-like visuals of your special day or giving your wedding a vintage look by shooting in 8 mm, we are dedicated to creating wedding films that are visual works of art. There are several things to consider. Some things that we offer that are unique to our company are Save the Date films, 3D photo montages and Same Day Edit films.

The Save the Date films will set the tone for your wedding. This allows your guests to get a sense of what they can expect on your wedding day.

One of the most popular offerings is our 3D photo montage, which offers a fresh new way of presenting you and your fiancé's most memorable moments. Our creative artists work with the same technology seen in hit 3D movies to bring your old pictures to life.

A Same Day Edit allows for your guests to experience the behind-the-scenes moments and relive the big day before they leave the reception.

How many cameras and camera operators typically film a wedding?

There are typically two filmmakers in order to capture action and reaction. It is important to not only film the bride walking down the aisle but also the groom's powerful and emotional reaction to seeing his beautiful bride walking down to join him. This is something a couple will want to relive over and over again.

At what pricing does a wedding coverage usually start, and what does a couple get for this price?

Having a film that allows you to relive and share your special day is priceless, but knowing all of the specifics is important. A well-commissioned film starts at $4,000, which includes eight hours on the wedding day, two filmmakers, 20-25 minute feature film and 40 hours of post-production time to bring all the elements together to showcase your story.

What is the customary procedure for placing a deposit and paying the balance?

Brides usually commission us 8-16 months before the wedding. A 50% retainer is placed to reserve the date, and the balance is due two weeks prior to the wedding. We understand that there are countless things to complete at this time so we strive to make our payment process as seamless as possible. You can pay electronically, or by check, cash and money order.

How do wedding videographers account for various lighting conditions?

" The camera captures light; our minds capture images." - *Anonymous*

We can't speak on the behalf of other filmmakers, but our team has an eye for lighting, and once one understands light, the real artistry begins. The possibilities with lighting are endless and can create the moods, themes and set the whole tone for the story and film.

When selecting a wedding videographer, what should a couple take into consideration?

First of all ask your married friends for recommendations; they are going to be your best resource.

Some things to take into consideration when you are looking for a wedding filmmaker are the steps or method they use to get to know you. Are they asking specific details of your wedding? Are they asking about you and your fiancé? Does it feel as if they genuinely care about your big day, or does it feel rushed? The filmmaker needs to know specifics so they can capture your story in a style that is unique to you and your fiancé.

What type of equipment should a good wedding videographer use?

Equipment is just a tool; it is the storytelling aspect that you should be after. When you watch a piece of work from a filmmaker, does it connect emotionally with you? If it does, then you know that person is a storyteller, and that is exactly what you want for the most important day of your life. A studio could be fully loaded with all of the newest technology and equipment, but without the creativity and artistry of a true filmmaker that equipment is just stuff.

What is the standard attire/dress for the wedding videographers, and can couples usually make special requests in this area?

This is a question that has to be asked because we do not want to be the ones standing out on your day. For instance, if a client is having a beach wedding we do not want to show up wearing black attire when everyone else is wearing light colors.

Is it customary to provide food for the videographers?

It is recommended that you provide a meal for your filmmakers because they are going to be there with you from the beginning to end. This does not mean you have to give them what the guests are having, but it is suggested to feed your filmmakers.

Is it typical for the wedding videographers to take breaks during the wedding? If so, how many breaks are standard, and how long should each break typically last?

Your filmmakers do not necessarily need a break, but there are times when it will make sense for a break, for example, at dinner. No one wants to be awkwardly filmed while eating, so this is a perfect opportunity for your filmmakers to take time to recharge.

How long does it usually take, after the wedding, for the couple to receive their wedding video?

This really depends on your commissioning. The same day edit is of course delivered that night, but it takes about 12-14 weeks to create a more comprehensive and amplified film.

If a couple wants certain things excluded from their wedding video, how and when should this be communicated to the wedding videographer?

We use a consultative approach so every detail is discussed and documented with your project manager. There are always things that come up last minute, so communicate any changes or exclusions to our team as soon as possible in order to assure that your film is going to be exactly the way you envision it.

You can contact Hakim Sons Films in any of the following ways:

Studio: 500 Crescent Court, Suite 100
Dallas, Texas 75201. Phone: (800) 713-8913
Email: info@hakimsonsfilms.com

15 THE WEDDING PHOTOGRAPHER

Your wedding photos can be taken only once. Therefore it's important to talk to the photographer about all the different aspects that come into play. Are there any specific things the photographer should know about? What exactly do you get for the price you pay? Sometimes you pay for the photographer on your wedding day and pay for the chosen photos separately. Do you want to edit the photo's yourself or let the photographer create a professional album for you? These are all choices depending on the budget size. To make sure you get the best information about wedding photography, we interviewed Jessica D'Onofrio from Jessica D'Onofrio Photography.

"At the heart of my style is the celebration of romance. Of poetry in the human spirit. Two lives unifying in one perfect moment, shared with all the faces most beloved to them in the world.

Tender hearts, joyful moments, and elegant simplicity. Cinematic portraits that show the tangible love between you, and the true dynamic of your relationship with one another.

I am a natural light, fine art photographer who travels the world capturing life's most precious moments. I specialize digital capture, edited for a classic film look."

What are the advantages of hiring a professional wedding photographer as opposed to having a friend or family member take the pictures?

This most obvious answer to this question is skill alone. Professional wedding photographers have years of experience honing their craft and defining their own unique aesthetic and style. They know every in and out of their equipment, which allows them to utilize them to their full capabilities. They've mastered light—how to use it, how to manipulate it, and how to make the most of it. It may seem as easy as picking up a camera and snapping a picture, but there is so much that goes into creating a truly beautiful image.

Some of that is technical aptitude and knowledge, and some of that is inherent talent and artistry. Mix these together, and that is just not a formula "Uncle Bob" has the capacity to recreate. But beyond this, even if Uncle Bob was, say... a fairly intermediate level amateur photographer, had a decent camera, and could take a pretty nice photo from time to time, chances are he has not been to hundreds of weddings. Why does this matter? A wedding is not like any other day. It is a day that is on a strict schedule, where rarely does everything go exactly as planned, without a hitch. Even a good everyday photographer will not always make a good wedding photographer.

A good wedding photographer is not only a skilled artist, they are adept at multitasking a dozen tasks at once, keeping everyone on schedule, and making sure that no spontaneous, once in a lifetime moment goes unseen. We have a long list of "must have" shots engrained into our brains that the average individual would most likely not even consider taking a photograph of, but a bride would be disappointed not to have. We know what kind of hiccups to anticipate during the day, and we have a solution for each of them. We don't look at each photograph we take as just an individual shot, we look at is as part of an entire storyline, and we already have a plan in place for how we want to tell that story. Not only to make sure that the moments are captured, but to make sure that when placed together in an album each of those images looks not only beautiful individually, but beautifully when placed together as well. We are not simply taking a snapshot of a dress, or shoes, or your mother hugging you; we are searching for the most beautiful way to do so.

The way in which the light hits you the most beautifully, feels the most natural, and elicits the most emotion. When your ceremony starts a half hour late because of a late bridesmaid, we know how to rearrange the time we're given for family formals to maximize our shortened time and still make sure you get all the portraits you wanted. It takes years of experience to understand the inner workings of a wedding day. It is a very hard job, and it can be extremely overwhelming for the average person. You have to always be on your toes, know exactly what comes next, and in the spare moments in between be watching for unexpected moments that you have no way of anticipating. You don't understand how to handle this with grace and ease until you've done it a few hundred times. That's an experience that even the most talented Uncle Bob just does not have.

Why do wedding photographers copyright the pictures they take at weddings? Is this common?
Well, let's say you wanted to hire a photographer. And let's say they were extremely generous and always gave their clients the copyright to their images, despite the fact that it goes completely against the industry standard. Now, let's say you asked them to see their portfolio so you can get a feel for their style. They can't show it to you. Why? Because they've released the copyright to their images, and now, those images are legally not theirs to show. Without retaining copyrights, photographers have no way to display, share, use, post, print, publish, or market those photographs. And who is going to hire a photographer that does not have one photo to show for themselves? That is the most basic reason. From there, we delve into issues of brand integrity and reputation. If a photographer sells the copyright to their images, then the buyer then has the right to do anything with those images that they please.

They can distribute them, and by doing so, other masses of people can then attain the original photographer's work and post it as their own. Perhaps someone posts it as their own and uses the images to build clientele that they treat poorly or scam; this can potentially negatively impact the reputation of the photographer. The photographer has no recourse. If, for some reason, the buyer wanted to sell them to a third party that ran some sort of non-PG business, they would have the right to do so. And the photographer's reputation and image would once more be negatively affected, but again, they would have no recourse. It could be argued that some photographers retain copyrights to have the flexibility to sell and market those images for their own profit (and they can legally do so), but the majority of photographers are focused on two very basic goals:

maintaining their portfolio and artistic integrity, and preserving their professional image.

Most wedding photographers will give you print release rights, which is the best of both worlds and generally agreeable between all parties. This simply means that you can take the photographers, print them, display them in your home, use them in wedding announcements, share them on Facebook, give them as gifts... the list goes on. Meanwhile, the photographer retains the copyright to make certain they are able to display and share their images while also preserving the integrity of them.

Is it better to book a wedding photographer who uses film or digital equipment?

There is no right or wrong answer to this question; it is purely subjective. Film and digital photographs produce two very distinct visual looks. One is not better nor worse than the other, they are simply... different. If one were to choose between two perfumes, it does not mean one is bad and one is good. It means simply that one is more suited to your taste. When choosing between them, the most important element to consider is simply which you prefer visually. Film typically gives a softer, dreamier quality to images, with absolutely gorgeous skin tones and a look that is very difficult to replicate digitally. The look of film is highly envied by many a digital photographer. The downside is that it is extremely expensive to shoot. This can often mean less overall photos taken at your wedding, and less overall images presented in your final package. It can often times mean a much larger investment.

Digital can also produce beautiful, high-quality images, and can do so cheaply and quickly. With the right equipment, it does not cost a digital shooter any more to shoot 2,000 images as it does to shoot 1,000. This gives them a much greater margin for error, as well as the ability to deliver a higher number of images. Someone who loves a dreamy, soft, organic quality to their photos may prefer the classic look of film. While someone who prefers extremely sharp, highly saturated, modern, glossy images may prefer the look of digital. It all comes down to your personal style. They are many photographers now who dub themselves "hybrid" shooters that will shoot portions of the day with a digital camera, and other portions of the day on film. Most of these will typically shoot the majority of their portraits on film. There are other photographers, like myself, who like to give clients the ease, convenience, and affordability of digital while ultimately providing the look of film. This is a look that is extremely hard to replicate digitally in post-production, and it takes many years of experience to get close, but when you are able to it is the very best of both worlds. For someone who is having a hard time deciding, I would suggest one of these final two options.

What is a proof and what are the advantages of the different types of proofing?

Most photographers consider "proofs" to be unedited versions of the images that they display to clients so that they can choose their favorites to be edited. Many wedding photographers will post hundreds of unedited images to a gallery following the event, and will give the client time to peruse these and choose a select few to then be edited. This works great for many photographers, and is still standard for a large majority in the wedding industry. However, in my opinion, the upgrades in post processing programs has made it so much easier to edit images quickly and efficiently, that for a wedding client, I don't find this extra step necessary any more.

Not only does it share your photos with you before they're perfect (which I think can be a bit disillusioning), but it also typically limits the amount of images the photographer is willing to give you fully edited. Wedding photographs are very different from something like a cosmetic ad. You are not choosing one key image to be displayed on a billboard where you need to erase every pore that ever existed. 30+hours of retouching is not necessary on each individual image. Generally with weddings, you are adjusting color, contrast, tone, and exposure with a few beauty retouches here and there to create a specific overall tone and continuity in the images. With programs like Lightroom available, there is no reason that every photo presented to you should not be at least lightly processed and retouched. Unless you are hiring a shoot and burn photographer, I find the need for classic "proofing" to be somewhat outdated and unnecessary in today's wedding photography market. Some photographers, however, have morphed the term to refer to their lightly retouched images as "proofs" while they still allow the client to choose from these for more intense editing. Make sure you clarify how they are using the term with your photographer.

What are the pros and cons of hiring two wedding photographers to take pictures at a wedding, as compared to only having one photographer taking pictures?

When speaking with potential clients, I liken it to watching a movie. If you were to watch a movie from one perspective, and one camera angle, for the entire duration, it would become extremely boring and redundant very quickly. There is a reason that movies are designed to show you the entire scope of any given scene. It gives you a sense of environment and perspective. It gives you a sense of being immersed in the moment and enjoying it from every vantage point. Much in the same way, one person can only capture one specific vantage point at a time. Walking down the aisle is a perfect example. Would you rather have one photographer, standing in one place, with one perspective; or, would you rather have two photographers shooting from two angles, one focused on the groom's face as the bride walks down the aisle and he sees her for the first time, and one focused on the bride's face as she sees him bursting with anticipation? Two photographers can give you a level of depth and diversity in your image that one person just simply cannot feasibly capture. Perhaps in the same moment the bride dances with her father, the mother of the bride holds her hand to her heart and sheds a tear. Wouldn't you rather have both of these simultaneous moments captured than one? They both capture the same physical moment in time, but they capture two very different perspectives of it.

Logistically, it also creates a much more harmonious flow to your day and makes certain no moment goes unnoticed. With one photographer, during the getting ready stage, they're constantly having to run back and forth between where the bride is, and where the groom is. When they're with the groom, who knows what amazing candid moments they're missing with the bride. But they're only one person, and there is nothing they can do about it. But with two photographers you can have one with each and make certain neither of those moments goes unnoticed or unphotographed.

What types of wedding packages do photographers typically offer?

Most photographers will typically offer a basic package that includes coverage for the wedding day itself, but nothing else. They will also generally offer packages which include portrait sessions and albums. Some even include printed goods, such as save the dates. Some will charge separately for print release rights. Many will also allow you to custom build a package to suit the needs of your particular wedding.

What is the customary deposit to put down, to reserve a photographer for a date?
When is the balance typically due?

Every photographer handles this differently. Almost all professional wedding photographers will charge a deposit to hold a wedding date for you for the simple reason that once they have held the date on their calendar, they begin turning other work away. By charging a deposit, they ensure that you are serious about hiring them for the date, and they are guaranteed that even if you cancel your wedding and they lose other work, they will at least make a portion of the income that they should have. For this reason, most deposits will be non-refundable. Some photographers require monthly payments until the balance is paid in full; others require an initial deposit and then final payment anywhere from a month prior up until the date of the wedding.

Nearly all photographers will require you to pay your balance in full prior to receiving full resolution copies of your photographs. Otherwise, there would be nothing to keep clients from receiving photos, making copies, and never paying. This is industry standard and just a way for the photographer to protect their work and livelihood. Expect to pay for your images before you physically receive them.

Why is there such a large price range among different wedding photographers?

As with anything, you get what you pay for. Just because two individuals are photographers does not mean they both have invested in the same level of equipment, have the same level of skill, the same level of experience, nor the same level of artistic talent. There are photographers that have been working for 30 years with high technical knowledge that are not particularly artistic and take technically accurate, but not necessarily beautiful or inspired photos. And then there are photographers that are artistically fantastic behind the camera but terrible at album design or post production. You are investing in the quality of the mixture of these skills, as well as what they are offering you within their packages. If you want a photographer that is amazing to work with, has beautiful work, is professional and prompt, makes you a better version of yourself in front of the camera, is highly in demand, well respected, highly recommend, only uses the very best equipment, has won a myriad of awards, and is the envy of all of your friends... expect to pay for it. If you want someone that is perfectly acceptable but produces images that are not particularly exceptional, then you might get a better deal.

At what point in the wedding planning process should a couple book a wedding photographer?
As soon as you have definitively settled on a date and contracted your venue. Good wedding photographers book a year or more in advance. For many brides, they are one of the most important investments they make in their wedding. You cannot carry around a cake or post a centerpiece on the wall. Your wedding photographs are the one thing you can display in your home, share on your phone, give as gifts, and enjoy casually in your day to day life, every day of your life. It is one of the most invaluable heirlooms you will ever have to share with your children and grandchildren. Because wedding photographers are contracted so far out, if you wait, they become less and less likely to be available. A bakery can bake more than one cake for a wedding day. A photographer can only accept one wedding. If you find a photographer whose work you love, whose ethic you respect, and whose personality you connect with, book them. In playing the field

and trying to find a better deal, they may be booked by someone else who is looking for quality over quantity before you have a chance to. Everyone gets a lower price on their second choice, but that doesn't make it a good deal. And every good photographer that respects their artistry always wants to book with the client that truly loves their work instead of the client that has to be convinced.

What should a couple look for in a wedding photographer?

You should love their images first and foremost. This goes without saying, and only you can decide for yourself what that special something is that you will connect with in photographs. If you've found that, the next step is to make sure they're within your budget and can offer the items you're looking for in your wedding package. Beyond this, you must absolutely, positively without doubt feel a connection and affinity to your photographer. It is very much like starting a relationship. It can look good on paper, but if the connection is not there, it just isn't going to work out.

This is your wedding day; your photographer is going to see you at your best and your worst, and if you're a bride, they will most likely see you in your skivvies! If you do not feel perfectly comfortable, at ease, and completely yourself with your photographer, it will absolutely without question show in your photographs. When you feel a connection to your photographer that allows them to feel like an old friend, you forget the camera is there. When you are naturally yourself and authentically you, you will look your very best on camera. These are the emotional, unobtrusive moments that tell your story, and you just cannot get them if you are constantly feeling uncomfortable. It sounds a bit cheesy, but you are hiring the person as much as you are hiring their work.

Who they are is equally as important as what they can produce, because it affects how you handle yourself in front of their camera. You should walk away from your consult feeling as though you've just made a new lifelong friend. If it was full of awkward silences and uncomfortable pauses, it's not a match. It is business, but it is also the start of a new relationship that will span 1-2 years of your life, minimum. Between engagement sessions, bridals, the wedding day, and building albums, you will be a part of each other's lives for quite a while, and it should be a blissful collaboration, not a bitter union.

What should a couple beware of with certain wedding photographers?

The most telling horror story I hear of within the industry is photographers that promised brides they would receive "all" of their edited images on disk, only for the brides to receive their final disk and indeed have all the final edits, but in thumbnail form with the photographer then insisting they would have to pay for large scale images. This is an argument over semantics, but it is a valid one. Make sure you understand exactly what it is that your photographer will be delivering to you. Approximately how many images? Will these be edited? How am I allowed to use these images? Will I receive them on disk? At what resolution? Having beautiful images is fantastic, but without knowing how you can actually possess them for your purposes, they're useless. You can't show your children a jpeg on a website 30 years from now.

How should a couple determine their wedding photography budget?

You should ask yourself this question: after my wedding, of all of the items I invest in, which can I physically posses as a keepsake to relive my day over and over again? Photography is indisputably one of the most important investments you can make in your wedding day. Your cake will be eaten. Your dress will be stored in a closet. People will forget exactly how the food tasted. The flowers will wilt, and the gifts will be put away. Images are one of the few tangible items you will be able to keep with you to enjoy over and over through your life. You will be able to share them with your children, and with their children. They will bring you back to the moment and allow you to reexperience it over and over again. When you are allocating what percentage of your budget will go to what area, consider this fact. Which parts of your wedding day can you share with your children and grandchildren? Will they taste your cake? Will they smell the flowers? Now ask yourself, will they enjoy the photos and experience a moment they perhaps were not even alive to be a part of? This is how important your wedding photography is in relation to the other aspects of the day. When allocating your budget, decide it based upon priority and not only what will allow you to best enjoy the moment in the moment, but what will allow you to enjoy the moment for the most prolonged period of time (like an entire lifetime).

What equipment should a wedding photographer have?

There is the age old battle between Nikon and Canon. There is no right or wrong. The majority of today's high-end camera equipment is top notch. You should never worry yourself over a debate between brands. You do, however, want to make certain that whatever brand they choose, that they are using the professional-grade equipment available in this brand. It is also extremely important that your photographer (and their assistant) not only carry one professional grade camera body on them, but a backup as well. Technology is not failsafe, and through no fault of their own, cameras can fail without warning. They should absolutely always have professional-grade equipment, with backups of not only their camera bodies, but additional lenses beyond their primary lens as well.

Do prices typically vary for off-season or weekday weddings?

Every photographer has a different policy. For most, you are paying for their time, and it has a value, whether it be on a Monday or a Saturday. The day of the week (or time of year) does not change that they are at your event shooting for a specific period of time, and then spending a specific period of time in post processing editing your photos. If the amount of time spent is equal, why would the payment not also be equal? I think it is perfectly acceptable for a photographer to charge for the value of their work regardless of when they are shooting. But, some photographers will offer smaller packages with less hours for a lower rate for weekday or off-season events. You may pay a lower price, but will likely also be getting a smaller package.

Is it possible to get black and white photographs as well as color photographs, or do couples typically have to decide between one or the other?

If you choose a film photographer and ask them to shoot some of your images (or they are known to shoot some of their images) in black and white, you have made a choice. Those images cannot then be converted into color. Their color images, however, can. If you have hired a digital shooter, you have the flexibility to receive either color or black and white versions of specific images. Whether your photographer provides those to you is up to their own discretion.

You can contact Jessica D'Onofrio Photography in the following ways:

www.jessicadonofrioweddings.com
jessica@jessicadonofrio.com

Pro-Motion Publishers

CONCLUSION

Congratulations! You now have the combined knowledge that all of our interviewees have been generous enough to share! We hope that you now feel confident and excited to go out and plan your special day. Before you get started, though, we'd just like to share a little more advice with you:

In all likelihood, you are only going to have one wedding. This also means that you're also only going to have one time in your life when you are planning your wedding. Our advice to you is to not make the big day the only fun part. We truly hope that you enjoy the process of planning your wedding as much as you enjoy your wedding day.

All too often in life, we put all of our focus on the end result, and we lose sight of the fact that the journey, not just the destination, should be exciting and enjoyable too. We hope that you find enjoyment in your wedding planning journey. We hope that you cherish each moment of planning your wedding, even if unexpected things still happen along the way. Always remember that life would be boring if everything always went exactly as expected. When unexpected things happen, try to smile and accept it as part of the journey.

We have done our best to compile the best advice that we were able to find, from true wedding industry professionals. Even though you now have a substantial advantage over couples who plan their weddings without the knowledge that you now have, there are still bound to be some bumps in the road, in the days leading up to your big day. As with all things in life, it's not what happens to you throughout the wedding planning process, it's how you handle those things that happen to you along the way. Embrace the challenges and welcome the unexpected. Each challenge that you resolve will bring you one step closer to your big day.

We wish you all the best as you plan your wedding. May you find happiness, excitement, and fun in all of the days leading up to your wedding, and beyond!

Made in the USA
Lexington, KY
04 April 2016